W9-BCC-800

ART:
Choosing and Expressing

GUY HUBBARD
Head of Art Education, Indiana University

MARY J. ROUSE
Professor of Art Education, Indiana University

BENEFIC PRESS   WESTCHESTER. ILLINOIS

Front Cover
"Untitled, 1960" by Lee Bontecou
Courtesy of The Art Institute of Chicago

Lee Bontecou is a very original American artist. She makes pictures that are also partly relief sculpture. She mixes art materials together, such as metal and canvas, in new and strange ways. She never tries to make her work look realistic and she doesn't give titles to her art. She believes that people should enjoy the art just because it is interesting and not because it makes them think of something they have seen before.

Title Page
"Place of Darkness" by Abraham Rattner
Courtesy of the Indiana University Art Museum

Abraham Rattner is an American artist. This painting shows things that we can recognize, but they are distorted and the colors are very strange — just as they might be in a nightmare. In this way the artist gives us a much stronger feeling of mystery and fear than if he had painted the picture realistically.

Back Cover
"Peasant of the Camargue" by Vincent Van Gogh
Courtesy of the Fogg Art Museum, Harvard University
Bequest of Grenville L. Winthrop

Most people draw with pencils. But when they use pen and ink, the lines are usually thin. In this drawing, Vincent Van Gogh used a pen that made very thick lines. Instead of filling in all the spaces with shading, he put lines and dots only in the spaces where he needed them.

Even though the style of drawing is different from what other artists do, this picture tells you all you need to know about this old man who has lived all his life working hard on a farm.

Library of Congress
Number 76-23707
ISBN 0-8175-0018-9

Copyright 1977 by Benefic Press
All Rights Reserved
Printed in the United States of America

2

CONTENTS

HOW TO USE THIS BOOK

To The Students

This book is not like most books. You don't read it from beginning to end. Instead, you pick out what you would like to do. Your teacher will also help you whenever you need it. But you will choose which lessons you do.

The Lessons

Every lesson fills two pages. Each one has the same parts to it. These parts are always shown in the same place on the page. Once you get used to the way each lesson is arranged, you should be able to work on your own most of the time. The lessons are not difficult to read. Your teacher will help you if you do not understand something.

Start at the top left page. The first thing you will see is a strand. A strand is a drawing of circles, squares, and diamond shapes joined together by lines. These strands are explained later in this introduction.

Next you will see the lesson number and title. It gives you some idea of what is in the lesson. The sentences that follow the title tell you more about the lesson.

Below this are the instructions for what to do. The pictures that go with the lesson are also to help make the lesson easier to understand. You will often see a sentence that tells you where to find explanations for some of the special art words that are used. This word list, or Glossary, is on pages 232-236, near the back of the book. In addition there may be a sentence telling you where to find out how to do something. The How To Do It section is on pages 237-250.

In many lessons there are references to the works of great artists. On pages 9-11 you will find an alphabetical list of these artists and some information about them. Following this listing is a section of reproductions of masterpieces. These masterpieces are also referred to in the lessons, followed by a number and letter in parenthesis. The number indicates the page and the letter tells you where on the page the artwork appears.

At the bottom of the facing page is a list of the things you will have learned by doing the lesson. The first kind are things to understand and remember. The second kind is about making things in art. The third kind is about appreciating art and deciding what you like. A letter at the end of each sentence tells you more about what you will have learned. An (A) is about learning to see. A (B) is about the meanings of words. A (C) has to do with knowing things about art. A (D) is about deciding what you like. An (E) is about using materials and tools properly. An (F) tells you what art you will make.

Next to this section is a box. It shows a list of art materials you can use for the lesson. You may want to use other materials, but ask your teacher first.

The Kinds of Art

To help you choose the kinds of art you want to do, there is a section at the back of the book called Index of Art You Want To Do. This index is arranged alphabetically by subject, such as; Animals, Architecture, Collage, etc. A description of specific skills and lesson numbers follows each listing, such as: Animals — a collage of an animal — lesson 30.

The Strands

Whenever you choose to do something from this book, it will always be part of a group of lessons. These groups of lessons are called strands. When you have decided what to do, you begin at the left side with the first lesson in the strand. Sometimes a lesson you really want to do does not come first. But it is best to do the lessons in the order they come in the strand.

Every lesson in the book shows a picture of the strands that lesson is in. Every strand has a name to help you know what it is about.

The strands are all shown the same way. You can find a list of all the strands in the book on page 29. There is a picture of one of them at the bottom of this page.

Follow along with these directions:
1. Begin at the left side. The lesson numbers are shown inside circles. The lessons you can choose from here are numbers 76 and 29. Choose one lesson.
2. Do the lesson you chose. When your teacher is satisfied with your work, you are ready to do another lesson.

3. The next lessons to choose from are shown in square boxes. In this strand they are numbers 20, 70, and 53. Choose any one of these three lessons.
4. Do the lesson you like best. Always ask your teacher for help if you need it. When your teacher has made sure you have done the work properly, you are ready to do the third lesson. Strands all have three lessons.
5. The third lesson is number 92. You cannot choose any other lessons this time.
6. Last of all is a short lesson to help you judge your art. It shows a small letter inside a diamond shape. All of the things you have to do in these strand endings are described on page 31. Every strand ends with one of these judging lessons. The strand is finished only when you do this last part properly.

These are the only things you have to remember when you use this art book. If you work quickly you can do more lessons than if you work slowly. But the important thing is to do good work. The book is meant to be used by you so you can do the art you enjoy most of all. Then you will learn more.

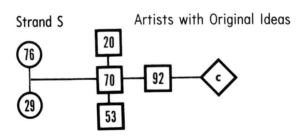

Strand S   Artists with Original Ideas

ARTISTS' REFERENCE

Artist	Style; Technique
Benton, Thomas Hart (1889-1975)	Mural painter and printmaker who specialized in American country life and mountain people.
Bierstadt, Albert (1830-1902)	Landscape painter who traveled across the West with wagon trains, doing views of the mountains and prairies.
Braque, Georges (1882-1963)	French abstract painter who also made collages.
Breughel, Pieter (C. 1525/30-1569)	European (Flemish) painter and draftsman who interpreted the older art tradition of his country in a new way.
Cézanne, Paul (1839-1906)	French painter who studied the actual construction of objects and how they fit together in pictures. He painted landscapes and still lifes.
Chagall, Marc (1887-)	Russian painter who makes dream-like scenes that remind us of surrealist art.
Davis, Stuart (1894-1964)	American painter whose bold, bright colors of abstract art show things from everyday life.
Dürer, Albrecht (1471-1528)	German painter, engraver, and designer of woodcuts. Dürer is one of the greatest of all German visual artists.
El Greco (1541-1614)	Greek-Spanish painter, famous for his mysterious colors and distorted human figures.
Gauguin, Paul (1848-1903)	French painter, sculptor, ceramicist, and printmaker. He painted with simplified shapes, bright color and decorative patterns.
Hiroshige, Ando (1797-1858)	Japanese printmaker who specialized in landscapes following the success of Hokusai.
Hokusai (1760-1849)	Japanese printmaker who trained as a woodblock engraver. He also invented a new style of landscape painting.
Holbein, Hans (1497-1543)	German painter and designer of woodcuts who painted portraits and religious pictures.
Hopper, Edward (1882-1967)	American artist whose work in oil and watercolors illustrated scenes in towns and cities in the eastern part of the United States.
Hurd, Peter (1904-)	American painter, illustrator, and printmaker. His detailed tempera paintings are of figures and landscapes in the cattle country of the Southwest.
Huysum, Jan van (1682-1749)	Dutch painter who was thought of as one of the greatest flower painters.
L'Enfant, Pierre Charles (1754-1825)	French engineer and architect, who was the first modern city planner, responsible for planning Washington, D. C.

Leonardo da Vinci (1452-1519)	Italian painter, sculptor, architect, engineer, and scientist. He was one of the greatest painters of the Italian Renaissance.
Lindner, Richard (1901-)	German-American painter whose art criticized life in Germany in the 1920's and later, the pop art of the United States.
Marin, John (1870-1953)	American artist whose clear, vividly colored watercolors of New York and the New England coast showed movement and feeling through angular lines.
Matisse, Henri (1869-1954)	French painter who worked with bright colors and patterns that were full of movement. His pictures are mainly about people and still lifes.
Michelangelo (1475-1564)	Great Italian Renaissance painter and sculptor, best known for his masterpieces showing the human body.
Miró, Joan (1893-)	Spanish painter, printmaker, ceramicist, and scenic designer. Miró is an abstract surrealist artist.
Moore, Henry (1898-)	English sculptor whose art objects of wood and stone seem to be shaped by natural forces.
Monet, Claude (1840-1926)	French impressionist painter. Monet painted with dabs of bright color that seem to come together when you stand back and look at them from a distance.
O'Keeffe, Georgia (1887-)	One of the first leaders of modern American paintings. Her pictures are usually about New Mexico.
Orozco, José Clemente (1883-1949)	One of Mexico's best known painters whose work shows powerful feelings and a dramatic style.
Picasso, Pablo (1881-1973)	Born in Spain, Picasso lived in France, where he led the world in painting and drawing the complicated ideas of the twentieth century.
Pollock, Jackson (1912-1956)	American painter who made pictures by dribbling paint onto canvas; he was an important abstract expressionist painter.
Rembrandt (1606-1669)	Dutch painter of history, portraits, landscapes, and house interiors. Rembrandt was also a draftsman and printmaker. His paintings showed dark shadows with usually only one part brightly lit.
Remington, Frederic (1861-1909)	American artist who captured the spirit of the West in his paintings, drawings, and sculptures of cowboys and Indians.
Renoir, Pierre (1841-1919)	French impressionist painter and sculptor, who learned the impressionist way of working from Monet. Renior painted figures in outdoor scenes.
Rivera, Diego (1886-1957)	Famous Mexican mural painter whose favorite subjects were revolution and work.

10

Russell, Charles M. (1864-1926)	American painter and sculptor who worked in pen and ink, oil, watercolor, and clay, to show scenes about cowboys of the West.
Sedgley, Peter (1930-)	American painter and sculptor who produces interesting effects through different ways of using color and line.
Seurat, Georges (1859-1891)	French painter who invented pointillism. Colors are painted in small dabs; our eyes unite them.
Shen Chou (1427-1509)	Chinese painter and poet. He was one of the greatest artists while the Ming emperors ruled China.
Siqueiros, David (1896-1974)	Mexican mural painter whose work is about political, and industrial changes. He used a mixture of realism and fantasy.
Sisley, Alfred (1839-1899)	English born, impressionist painter. Sisley painted mostly landscapes around Paris.
Tamayo, Rufino (1899-)	Mexican artist whose paintings of human figures and still lifes are colorful and abstract.
Titian (c. 1487/90-1576)	One of the greatest masters of the Italian Renaissance. He painted people and historical stories. Titian lived in Venice.
Turner, Joseph M. (1775-1851)	English landscape painter who used oils and watercolors. Turner had a great understanding of the effects of light and developed this in his paintings.
Van Gogh, Vincent (1853-1890)	Dutch artist who used lines as well as thick paint to create his colorful paintings, that are full of movement.
Vasarely, Victor (1908-)	French painter whose work explores the artistic ideas that are possible in geometric shapes. This is sometimes called Op art.
Weyden, Roger van der (1399-1464)	European (Flemish) painter who used new ways of designing pictures in the fifteenth century to make them have more feeling.
Wood, Grant (1892-1942)	American artist who painted scenes about Midwestern country life in a straightforward, simple manner.

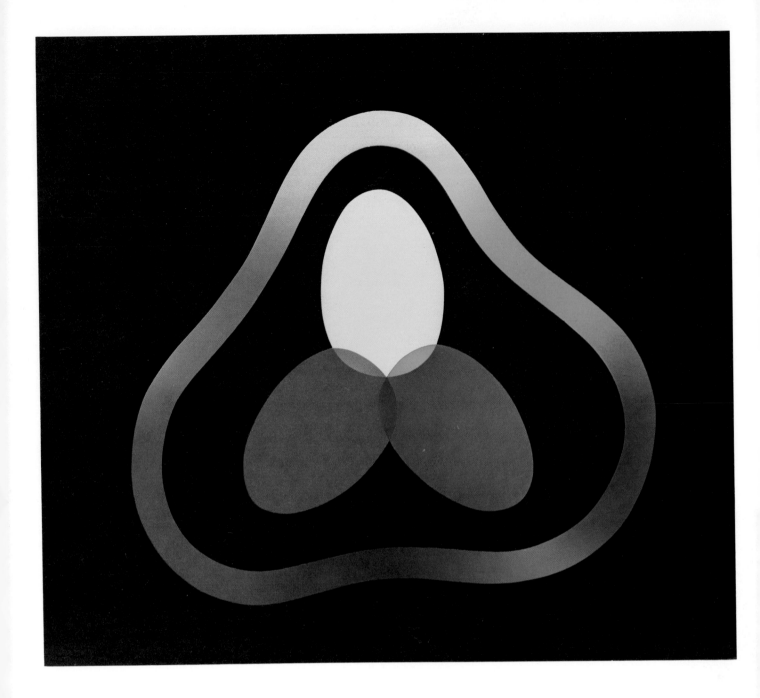

Much of the great art of the world is made up of color. This design shows the colors used by artists of every century and every place. There are three colors from which all other colors come. These are the primary colors — red, yellow, and blue. Find these colors on the color design. Notice all the varieties of color that come from them. Do you see green, orange, blue-green, purple? You probably can identify many other colors, too.

Works of Great Artists

On the following pages you will find reproductions of great works of art. All of these have been referred to in the lessons that you will be doing. Each artwork is identified by title and artist.

(A)

"June, 1975" by Nancy Singleton
Photograph by Kirk Ostby

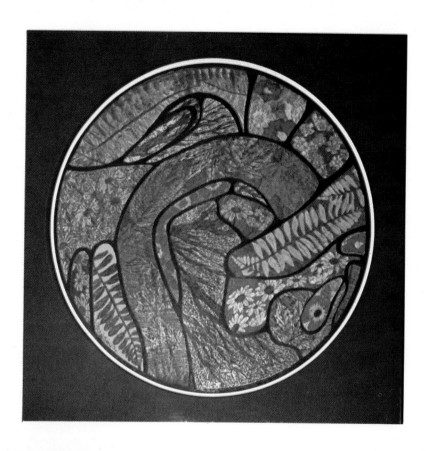

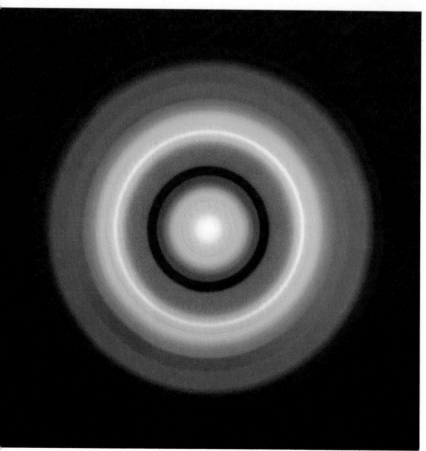

(B)

"Phantom" by Peter Sedgley (1930-   )
Courtesy of the Indiana University Art Museum

15

"Head of Woman" by Hans Holbein (1497-1543)
Trustees of the British Museum

16

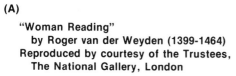

17

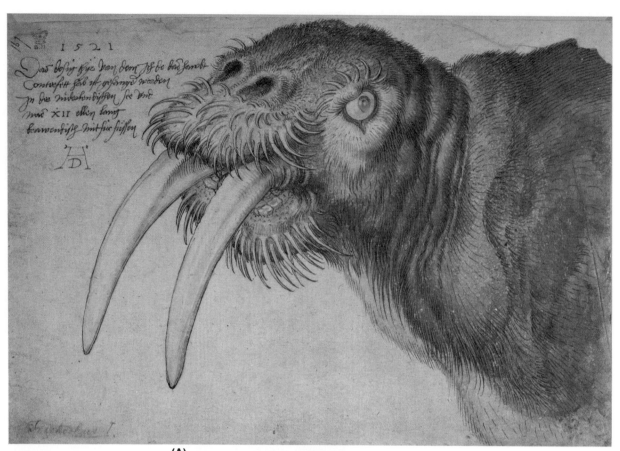

(A) "Head of Walrus" by Albrecht Durer (1471-1528)
Trustees of the British Museum

18

(B) "The Great Wave of Kanagawa Nami-ura" by Hokusai (1760-1849)
Trustees of the British Museum

19

(A) "Moonlit Night" by Ando Hiroshige (1797-1858)
Trustees of the British Museum

(B) "Peach Blossom Valley" by Shen Chou (1427-1509)
Trustees of the British Museum

(A) "Cliff Walk, Etretat" by Claude Monet (1840-1926)
Courtesy of The Art Institute of Chicago

(B) "San Marco" by Pierre Auguste Renoir (1841-1919)
The Minneapolis Institute of Arts

"The Starry Night" by Vincent Van Gogh (1853-1890)
(1889)
Oil on canvas, 29" x 36¼"
Collection, The Museum of Modern Art, New York.
Acquired through the Lillie P. Bliss Bequest.

(A) "Tahitian Landscape" by Paul Gauguin (1848-1903)
The Minneapolis Institute of Arts

(B) "Rue a Moret sur Loing" by Alfred Sisley (1839-1899)
Reproduced by permission of the Syndics of the
Fitzwilliam Museum, Cambridge

24

(B) "Burning of the Houses of Parliament, 1834" by Joseph Mallord William Turner (1775-1851)
The Cleveland Museum of Art, Bequest of John L. Severance

(A) "Interior with Etruscan Vase" by Henri Matisse (1869-1954)
The Cleveland Museum of Art, Gift of Hanna Fund

25

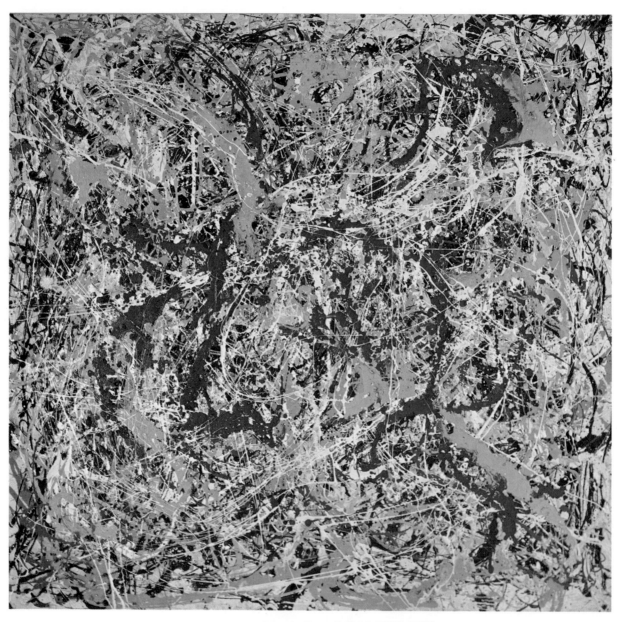

"Number 11" by Jackson Pollock (1912-1956)
Courtesy of the Indiana University Art Museum

(A) "Person Throwing a Stone at a Bird" by Joan Miro (1893-1926)
1926
Oil on canvas, 29″ x 36¼″
Collection, The Museum of Modern Art, New York. Purchase.

(B) "The Soldier Drinks" by Marc Chagall (1897-   )
1912
The Solomon R. Guggenheim Museum, New York

27

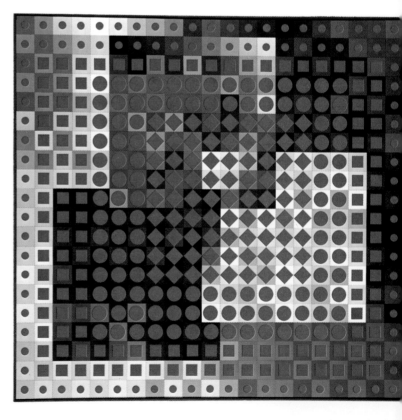

THE STRANDS

Strand	First Lesson(s)	Strand Title
A	71, 84	Distorting Faces
B	63, 6	Sculptors and Sculpture
C	68	Constructed Sculpture
D	11, 10	Daydreams and Nightmares
E	10	Giving the Feeling of Distance
F	15	Creative Ideas
G	31, 62	Getting Ideas from Other Artists
H	30	Architecture is Art
I	17, 15	Different Ways of Seeing
J	81	Unusual Ideas for Art
K	13	Careful Observation
L	53	Showing Strong Feelings in Art
M	49	Putting People in Your Art
N	88	Lines in Sculpture
O	1, 79	Faces
P	43, 77	Lines and Design
Q	29	Action and Abstract Art
R	49	People at Work and Play
S	76, 29	Artists with Original Ideas
T	68	Stitchery, Geometry, and Sculpture
U	9, 6	More Constructed Sculpture
V	55, 87, 46	Using What You See and Know
W	33, 51	Modeling and Carving
X	5, 96	Ideas from Sculptors
Y	25, 81, 7	Lines and Dots
Z	91, 89	Inspiration from Black Americans
AA	64, 71	Seeing and Doing Things Differently
BB	11, 25	Places You Know
CC	18, 17	Experiments with Light and Shadow
DD	22	Weaving and Stitchery
EE	88	Abstract Designing
FF	46, 13	More Careful Observation
GG	90, 25	Studies of Contours
HH	2, 54	The Ways Artists Look at Things

HOW TO FOLLOW A STRAND

1. All lessons fit into strands, so decide which one you want to do. Draw a picture of that strand on an evaluation sheet and put your name on it. Give the paper to your teacher to keep for you.

2. Read the first lesson in your strand very carefully. Be sure you understand exactly what to do. Ask your teacher to explain any parts you do not understand. Look at the Glossary if you do not know a word. Check the How To Do It section if you are unfamiliar with any activities.

   Look at the pictures that go with this lesson. They will help you understand what to do. Do not copy these pictures unless the lesson tells you to.

   If you do these first things carefully, you will not have to do the lesson over again later. It is a good idea before you start work to go to your teacher and tell him or her what the lesson is about.

3. Do exactly what the lesson tells you to do. Do the very best work you can do. If your teacher thinks your work is not as good as it should be, you may have to do the lesson again.

   If you need any help with your work, ask your teacher.

4. When you have finished, read the instructions again to be quite sure you have really done everything. Then show your work to your teacher. Look at your work with your teacher. Find out if you have done all the objectives. Find out if your artwork is good enough.

5. When your lesson is finished properly, put it up on the wall. Write the objectives you did clearly on a piece of paper and put it beside your artwork so other people will know what you learned.

6. Ask your teacher for the evaluation sheet that shows the picture of the strand you chose. Pick out the second lesson. Do it in the same way as the first lesson.

   When the second lesson is done, do the third one.

7. After you have done three lessons properly, you will be at the end of your strand. There is a diamond shape with a letter inside ($\langle a \rangle$, $\langle b \rangle$, $\langle c \rangle$, $\langle d \rangle$).

   Do the strand ending for your strand. Do it as well as you can. Your teacher will tell you if it is good enough.

   When this is done you are ready to look for another strand.

STRAND ENDINGS

Every strand is made of lessons you can choose from. You do three lessons to finish a strand. These lessons are all linked together. Some strands are on painting. Others are on being creative. After the three lessons in a strand are completed, it is good to think about what you have learned. That is what happens when you get to the diamond shape with the letter in it. There is one of these shapes at the end of every strand. Here is what you do:

 When you see a diamond shape with an "a" inside it, you are to pick out one of the things you did in that strand. All art means something. It may be about something that is fun. Or it may give you a feeling of being scared. The art may remind you of something you have seen before, or something in a dream you had.

Find the artwork that you can talk about best of all. Decide on all the meanings that you think show in it. Then tell your teacher about every one of these meanings. If you prefer, write them down.

 When you see a diamond shape with a "b" inside it, you are to look at all the art that you did in that strand. Decide what art you learned from that strand. Also decide what art you used in that strand that you already knew. Try and think of every single thing that you learned or that you knew already— even how to sharpen a pencil. Tell your teacher about all the art you learned and all the art you knew already. You can write these things down instead, if you prefer.

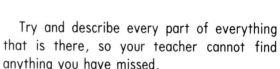 When you see a diamond shape with a "c" inside it, you are to look at all the art that you did in that strand. Pick out the best thing you did. Then describe to your teacher everything you can see in it. Don't leave out anything. Talk about the big shapes and little shapes. Talk about the different colors, and how they are different, and where they are different. Talk about the things in your art you can see, such as cats and clouds and flowers.

Try and describe every part of everything that is there, so your teacher cannot find anything you have missed.

 When you see a diamond shape with a "d" inside it, you are to look at all the work you did in that strand. Find the part you think is the best work you did in the whole strand. Decide why it is best. Next find the part you think is the worst you did. Decide why it is the worst.

One artwork may have the best as well as the worst parts in it. Or the whole artwork might be the best and another one might be the worst. And the best part could also show in more than one artwork, if that's what you think.

When you have decided what to say, tell your teacher. But don't just point to the two parts. Think of why the parts are best and worst. You can write these things down instead, if you prefer.

Strand K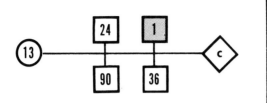

Strand O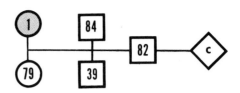

Lesson 1 — OLD AND YOUNG PEOPLE

Old people and children are not shown as often in art as people who are very strong or very beautiful. This lesson makes you think about how old people and children look. The pictures with this lesson are by famous artists and they show old and young people.

Instructions

1. Look at the picture of the child. Notice how round the face is. Notice how smooth the skin is and how big the eyes look.

2. Next look at the picture of the old man. Notice how pulled-in the face is. Notice how wrinkled the skin is and how small the eyes are.

3. Now draw two faces on one sheet of paper. Be sure that both faces are fairly big on your paper. Make one face look like a young girl or boy. Make the other face look like an old man or woman. Remember the big differences in the faces of old and young people. You might want to draw people you know, or you can make up the faces.

4. The color pictures by Pieter Breughel (14A), Leonardo da Vinci (15A), Titian (15B), Roger van der Weyden (17A), and Rembrandt (17B) all show how old and young people look.

Jean-Baptiste Perroneau, "Girl with a Kitten"

Reproduced by courtesy of the Trustees, The National Gallery, London

32

Albrecht Dürer, "Artist's Father"

Lesson Objectives

UNDERSTANDING ART (Conceptual)

Learn what differences there are in the faces of old and young people. (A)

MAKING ART (Performance)

a. Draw the face of an old person. (F)

b. Draw the face of a young child. (F)

| **Art Materials** |
| Drawing paper |
| Pencil and eraser |

33

Strand E

Strand I

Strand HH

Lesson 2 — FADE OUT

Colors sometimes just seem to fade away. It can happen on a foggy morning. It can happen when you squint your eyes in bright sunlight, or it can happen when you daydream. You can make colors fade on purpose with pencil lines and paint by making objects grayer and grayer as they fade into the distance.

Instructions

1. Draw in all the lines for a picture of a place where things seem to fade into the distance. It could be a smoky factory or a rainy day. Think up your very own idea for a picture to fill your paper.

2. Now lightly erase the pencil lines in your picture to make things that would look blurry not too easy to see clearly.

3. Paint your picture, but use only one color. Add very small dabs of black to your color to make it darker. Gray your paint(†) using black and white together. Things become grayer and less colorful in the distance. Painting with one color like this is called monochrome*.

4. The pictures that go with this lesson can help to make your artwork better. Look at them to help you think of other ideas. The color pictures by Shen Chou (20B), Paul Cezanne (21B), and Hiroshige (20A) all show scenes that fade into the distance.

* The meaning of this word is in the Glossary. (232-236)   † For an explanation turn to the How To Do It section. (237-250)

John Cotman, "Durham"

The Tate Gallery, London

34

Rockwell Kent, "Adirondacks" (34.4)

In the collection of the Corcoran Gallery of Art

Claude Monet, "London"

Reproduced by courtesy of the Trustees,
The National Gallery, London

Lesson Objectives
UNDERSTANDING ART (Conceptual)
    Learn how a monochrome painting is made. (C)
MAKING ART (Performance)
    a. Draw in all the lines for a picture of a place that is misty or smoky. (F)
    b. Make a picture to fill the paper. (F)
    c. Paint a monochrome picture. (F)
    d. Mix black and then white with a color to make different kinds of lightness and darkness. (E)
    e. Mix black and white together with a color to make it grayer. (E)
APPRECIATING ART (Affective)
    Decide which parts of a picture would be difficult to see clearly, and lightly erase those lines. (A)

Art Materials
White paper
Water, paper towels, etc.
Tempera paints
Brushes
Mixing trays
Pencil and eraser

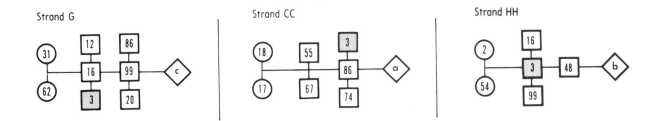

Strand G

```
31      12      86
        16      99      ◇ c
62       3      20
```

Strand CC

```
18      55       3
        86              ◇ a
17      67      74
```

Strand HH

```
 2      16
         3      48      ◇ b
54      99
```

Lesson 3 — THE DIFFERENT PARTS OF AMERICA

Some American artists paint scenes and subjects from their own part of the country. Thomas Hart Benton and Grant Wood painted pictures about the Midwest and the great prairie farms. Georgia O'Keeffe paints pictures about the Southwestern cattle country and deserts. Other artists live and work in different parts of America. They tell us something special about those places and the people who live there.

Instructions

1. Make your own picture of your part of America. Look around you to get ideas.

2. Draw and paint your picture using some of the ways these artists did their work.

Georgia O'Keeffe, "The Grey Hills"

Indianapolis Museum of Art, Gift of Mr. and Mrs. James W. Fesler

Thomas Hart Benton, "July Hay"

The Metropolitan Museum of Art, George A. Hearn Fund, 1943.

Grant Wood, "Stone City, Iowa"

Joslyn Art Museum, Omaha, Nebraska

Lesson Objectives
UNDERSTANDING ART (Conceptual)
  a. Learn that Georgia O'Keeffe paints pictures of the Southwestern deserts. (C)
  b. Learn that Grant Wood painted pictures of the Midwest. (C)
  c. Learn that Thomas Hart Benton painted pictures of prairie farms. (C)
MAKING ART (Performance)
  Make a picture about your own part of America. (F)
APPRECIATING ART (Affective)
  Choose some ways of painting from the art of Benton, O'Keeffe or Wood. (D)

Art Materials
White paper
Pencil and eraser
Paints
Brushes
Water, paper towels, etc.
Mixing trays

37

Strand H

Strand W

Lesson 4 — GREEK AND ROMAN ARCHITECTURE

Two thousand years ago the Greeks built great cities. The most famous city was Athens. The Greeks built beautiful palaces and handsome temples. Later, the Romans conquered the Greeks and copied their architecture. Afterward, the Romans invented their own style of building. Even today you will find many buildings that still use ideas first thought of by the Greeks and Romans.

Greek temples had slanted roofs like we have today, but theirs were made of stone. The heavy stone roofs had to be held up with many stone posts called columns*. All the Greek buildings had flat-topped arches*. Roman architects invented round arches and domes*. Greek and Roman architects carved beautiful decorations and sculptures to go on their buildings.

Instructions

Take a large lump of clay(†) and model it into the shape of a Greek or Roman temple. Put as much detail into the carving as you can. If you hollow out the inside of the lump of clay, you will be able to make a bigger model with the same amount of clay. If your model is of a ruined building, try to make it look as you think it did when it was first built.

*The meaning of this word is in the Glossary. (232-236)   † For an explanation turn to the How To Do It section. (237-250)

Pantheon, Rome

Parthenon, Athens

Model of the Parthenon

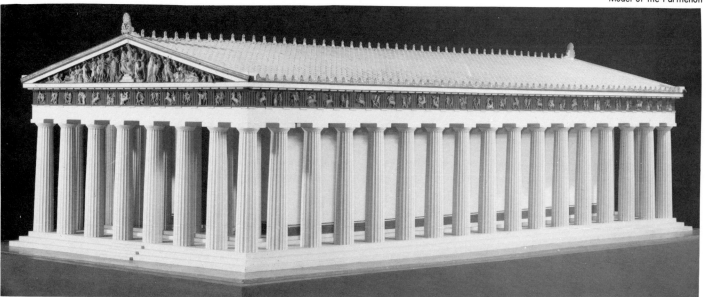

The Metropolitan Museum of Art, Levi Hale Willard Bequest, Purchase, 1890.

Lesson Objectives

UNDERSTANDING ART (Conceptual)

a. Explain the meaning of architecture as the art of designing and constructing buildings. (B)

b. Explain the meaning of an arch as an opening in a wall for people or light to pass through. (B)

c. Explain the meaning of a column as a post that holds up a roof. (B)

d. Explain the meaning of a dome as a curved roof that looks like a ball cut in half. (B)

MAKING ART (Performance)

a. Make a clay model of a Greek or Roman building. (F)

b. Show all the details you can see in your model. (A)

Art Materials

Clay (water or oil based)
Newspaper
Water (if needed)
Kitchen knife
Pencil or nail (for details)

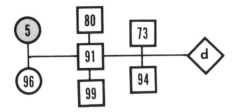

Lesson 5 — THE INSIDE OF SCULPTURE

Art made in school is usually small. Most pictures, drawings, and sculptures are made on desks and tables; but art doesn't have to be small. Palaces and cathedrals* are very big buildings. Many statues are much bigger than people. Giant paintings have been made that fill the ceiling and the walls of a room.

Instructions

1. Make a collection of interesting things for your sculpture.

2. Find a very large cardboard container. Turn it so that one side is open.

3. Use things from your collection to make the inside of the box look like a magic world. The inside walls will need things done to them to make them look like another world.

The open space* inside the box will need to be filled. You can stick(†) things on flat surfaces. You can decorate with painting and drawing, or with hanging things. Begin at the far inside of the box and gradually work outward.

4. The pictures that go with this lesson may help you get ideas for decorating your box.

*The meaning of this word is in the Glossary. (232-236) †For an explanation turn to the How To Do It section. (237-250)

Lesson Objectives

UNDERSTANDING ART (Conceptual)

a. Learn that good art is sometimes very big. (C)

b. Explain the meaning of space in sculpture as the open parts that are inside or between the solid pieces. (B)

MAKING ART (Performance)

a. Create sculpture to fill an open space. (F)

b. Attach objects so they will not come apart. (E)

APPRECIATING ART (Affective)

a. Show what a magical world might look like. (A)

b. Improve artwork with painting and drawing. (D)

Art Materials

Collection of fairly small items: bottles, boxes, egg cartons, cups, etc.

Large box

String, tape

Paints, brushes, scissors

Mixing trays

Water, paper towels

White and colored paper

Pencils and erasers, crayons

Glue and applicator

Strand B

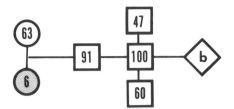

Strand U

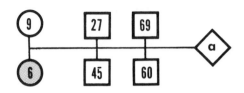

Lesson 6 — SYMMETRY

Paintings are flat, while sculpture isn't. Halfway between these two is something called a relief*. A relief is a picture that sticks out from a flat background. Look at the pictures that accompany this lesson.

Good art looks right because one side seems to balance the other. If things are exactly the same on each side, it is called symmetrical* balance. In this lesson you are going to make a symmetrical relief.

___

Instructions

1. Glue some of the things you have collected to fill a piece of cardboard. Arrange the pieces into a design you like. Experiment with different ways of building up the pieces so that they stick out at different distances. Be sure that they stick(†) firmly to the cardboard and do not fall off.

2. Be sure that the relief is balanced by being exactly the same on each side of the center line. Then it will be a symmetrical design.

3. When the glue is dry, paint your relief in one color so all the parts look as though they belong together. This is called unity*.

* The meaning of this word is in the Glossary. (232-236) † For an explanation turn to the How To Do It section. (237-250)

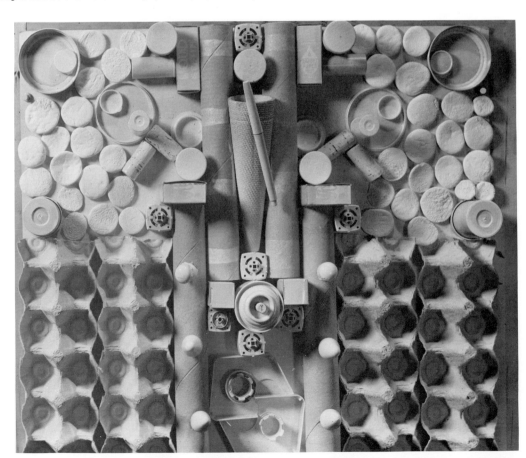

Lesson Objectives

UNDERSTANDING ART (Conceptual)

    a. Explain the meaning of the word relief in art as a kind of picture that sticks out from a flat background. (B)

    b. Explain the meaning of balance in art to be when all the parts of an artwork seem to be equal. (B)

    c. Explain the meaning of the word symmetry in art as a kind of balance. The things on each side of a center line are the same. (B)

MAKING ART (Performance)

    a. Make a symmetrical relief sculpture. (F)

    b. Attach objects so they will not come apart. (E)

    c. Paint sculpture all over in one color. (E)

APPRECIATING ART (Affective)

    Decide if your sculpture looks unified. (D)

Art Materials

A collection of small interesting-shaped objects that are usually discarded: flash cubes, bottle caps, small bottles, etc.

Glue and applicator

Paint, brushes

Cardboard or plywood, 12'' x 18'' or bigger

Mixing tray

Water, paper towels, etc.

Strand Y

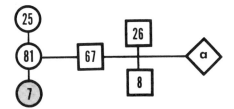

Lesson 7 — WANDERING LINES

Little children make scribble drawings without taking their pencils off the paper. The lines cross over and make shapes and the children color in the shapes. Artists draw without taking their pencils off the paper. Instead of scribbling, they draw things they know like pets, people, houses, and cars. That is what you will do in this lesson.

Instructions

1. Make a pencil drawing without taking your pencil off the paper. Your drawing will really be one big line. It is best to draw something that's right in front of you so you can see all its parts. It doesn't matter how many times you go over a part to get it right. The important thing is that you do not lift your pencil from the paper.

2. Look at your drawing and see which parts look best. Draw over the best parts with crayon, or pen and ink, or brush and ink (†). Remember that the finished drawing will show one heavy line; leave in the pencil lines.

3. The color picture by Jackson Pollock (26) shows a picture with wandering lines.

† *For an explanation turn to the How To Do It section. (237-250)*

Margaret Traherne, "Madonna & Child"

Pietro Da Cortona, "Death of Turnus"

Victoria and Albert Museum, Crown Copyright

Royal Library, Windsor Castle   Reproduced by Gracious Permission of Her Majesty The Queen.

Honoré Daumier, "A Clown"

The Metropolitan Museum of Art, Rogers Fund, 1927.

Lesson Objectives

UNDERSTANDING ART (Conceptual)

  Learn that artists often make drawings without ever taking their pencils off the paper. (C)

MAKING ART (Performance)

  Draw an object that is in front of you. Draw it without taking your pencil off the paper. (F)

APPRECIATING ART (Affective)

  Pick out the best pencil lines in your drawing. Make them show up with one crayon, pen, or brush line. (D)

Art Materials
White drawing paper
  9'' x 12'' or bigger
Pencil and eraser
Crayon
Pen and ink
Brush and ink (or thin paint)

45

Strand P

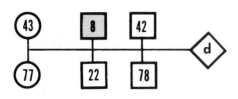

Strand Y

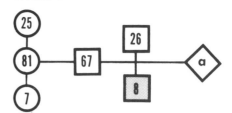

Lesson 8 — VISUAL ADJECTIVES

Some words mean special things to you. Words like crash, smile, drowning, touch, and hungry can remind you of something you have seen. It may be a very clear memory of something, or it could be something you have seen in your imagination. Some of these special words make pictures inside our heads. We can show them best through artwork.

Instructions

1. Think of words that mean special things to you. They should be words for the subjects of pictures you could make.

2. Make a drawing or painting that shows the best meaning of one of the words you thought
The meaning of this word is in the Glossary. (232-236)

of. Write the word at the bottom left corner of your work when it is finished. This is now the title* of your picture.

3. The color pictures by Hokusai (18B) and J.M.W. Turner (25B) show two special events.

David Alfaro Siqueiros, "Echo of a Scream". 1937. Duco on wood, 48" x 36".

Collection, The Museum of Modern Art, New York. Gift of Edward M. M. Warburg.

Clive Barker, "Splash" (Main View)

The Tate Gallery, London

Lesson Objectives

MAKING ART (Performance)
  a. List words that you could use for subjects for pictures. (C)
  b. Make a drawing from a word. (F)
  c. Explain the meaning of title in art as a name that describes the artwork. (B)

APPRECIATING ART (Affective)
  a. Decide on a word that would make a good picture. (D)
  b. Decide which art materials you like to use best. (D)
  c. Be sure your work is not like other people's. (A)

Art Materials
Drawing paper, 12" x 18"
Your choice: pen and ink, brush and ink, pencil, crayon, felt tip pen

47

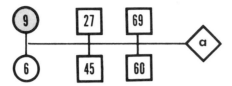

Lesson 9 — ART WITH HAMMER AND NAILS

All artists do things with their hands, but we don't usually think of making art with a hammer and nails. Yet people can make very good designs using nails pounded into wood. It may be a noisy way to make art, but the results can be very original*.

Instructions

1. Hammer lots of nails and tacks into a piece of wood to make a design. Pound some of them a long way into the wood; others can stick out. Some nails can be close together and others can be spread out. Pound some in straight and some in slanting.

Bend some of them on purpose. Use any other methods you can think of to make your design as original as you can.

2. A picture that sticks out like this at different heights is called a relief*.

* The meaning of this word is in the Glossary. (232-236)

Robert Seyle, "Nail Relief"

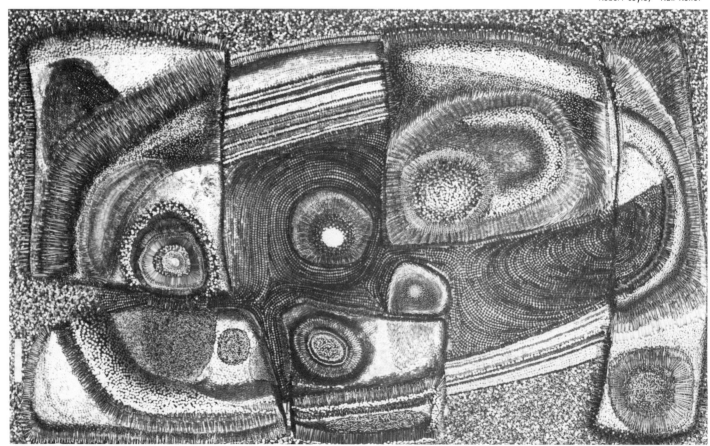

Ankrum Gallery, Los Angeles

Lesson Objectives

UNDERSTANDING ART (Conceptual)
  a. Explain the meaning of original in art as ideas that are very unusual or different. (B)
  b. Explain that a relief is a kind of art that sticks out from a flat background. (B)

MAKING ART (Performance)
  a. Pound nails into wood in all the different ways you can think of. (E)
  b. Make a relief design with nails pounded into wood. (F)

APPRECIATING ART (Affective)
    Decide if your relief looks original. (D)

Art Materials
A piece of plywood, 9″ x 12″ or bigger
Nails and tacks of different kinds
Claw hammer

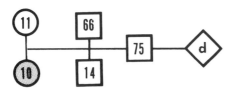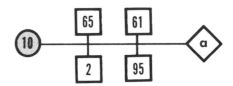
Lesson 10 — USING WATERY PAINT

Water is wet, drippy, blurry, and sometimes foggy. Pictures painted in watercolors* often look damp and soggy because lots of watery paint was used. This special effect is very useful when you want to make a picture that has a wet feeling.

Instructions

1. The first thing you should do is to make your paper wet with clean water. Then mop up any puddles on your paper before you begin to paint. Just dab up the puddles so that your paper is still wet.

2. Experiment on your paper with plenty of wet paint in your brush. Watch what happens to the paint. Try to make as many different effects as you can. Use as many sheets of paper as you need.

3. When the paper is dry, cut out the best effects you made. Stick them on a piece of paper(†) to make an interesting arrangement. The arrangement should exactly fill a square. Two words you can use instead of arrangement are design* and composition*.

4. The pictures that go with this lesson may help you to make your own artwork better. The color picture by Henri Matisse (25A) shows a painting done with very thin paint.

*The meaning of this word is in the Glossary. (232-236)   † For an explanation turn to the How To Do It section. (237-250)

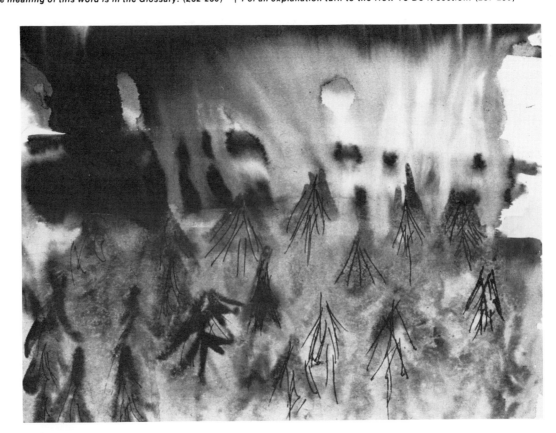

50

George Grosz, "Skyline of New York". 1934.

Watercolor on paper. 17 7/8 x 12 inches.
Collection of Whitney Museum of American Art.
Bequest of Miss Loula D. Lasker.

Finnish student

Learning Objectives

UNDERSTANDING ART (Conceptual)
a. Explain the meaning of watercolors as watery paints you can see through. (B)
b. Use the words composition and design instead of arrangement. (B)

MAKING ART (Performance)
a. Practice getting different effects with watercolors on wet paper. (E)
b. Cut out pieces of paper. (E)
c. Stick pieces of paper together firmly. (E)
d. Arrange pieces of paper to make an exact square. (A)

Art Materials
White paper, 12" x 18" or bigger
Big, soft brushes
Mixing tray
Scissors
Water, paper towels, etc.
Transparent watercolor paint
Paste and applicator

Strand D

Strand BB

Lesson 11 — DRY BRUSH

A brush full of wet paint makes a wet-looking painting. Quite a different effect happens with nearly dry paint on dry paper. The brush even makes a rustling, scratching sound as you paint. Dry brush painting is very useful when you want to make a picture with a dry feeling.

Instructions

1. Fill one sheet of paper with experiments using nearly dry paint. Find out how many different ways you can paint this way. Cut out (†) the experiments you think are best.

2. Next fill one sheet of paper with experiments using nearly dry paint. But first wet the paper with plenty of clean water. Find out how many different ways you can paint this way. When the paper is dry, cut out the effects you think are best.

3. Stick(†) all the cut-out pieces on a sheet of paper to make a collage*. They should be put together into a shape of something everyone can recognize. It could be a house, a horse, a person, or anything else you want.

4. The pictures that go with this lesson may help you, but use your own ideas. The color pictures by Pierre Renoir (22B) and J. M. W. Turner (25B) both show ways in which artists painted with brushes that were nearly dry.

*The meaning of this word is in the Glossary. (232-236)   † For an explanation turn to the How To Do It section. (237-250)

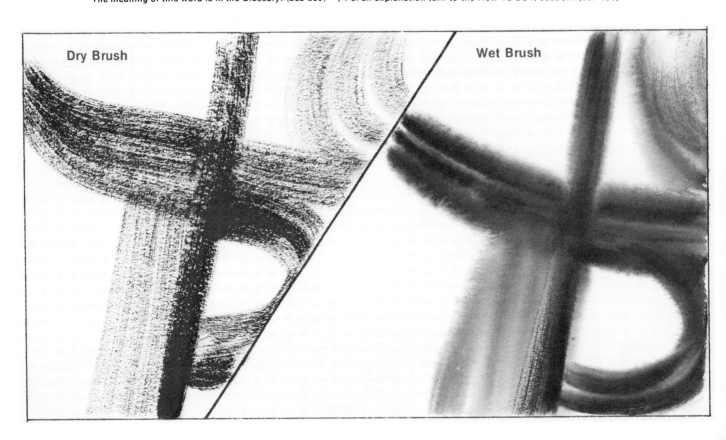

Dry Brush   Wet Brush

Lesson Objectives

UNDERSTANDING ART (Conceptual)
  a. Learn that nearly dry paint can be used to get special effects. (C)
  b. Explain the meaning of collage as art made by gluing things on a flat surface. (B)

MAKING ART (Performance)
  a. Practice getting different effects with nearly dry paint on dry paper. (E)
  b. Practice getting different effects with nearly dry paint on wet paper. (E)
  c. Stick pieces of paper together firmly. (E)
  d. Arrange the shapes so that they look like something you know. (A)

APPRECIATING ART (Affective)
    Pick out the best dry brush effects. (D)

Art Materials
White paper (12″ x 18″ or larger)
Medium-sized brush
Mixing trays
Scissors
Water, paper towels
Tempera paints
Paste and applicator

53

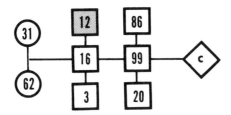

Lesson 12 — FARMS AND PLANTATIONS

The early settlers changed the land. They built homes. They cleared the land of trees and made farms and plantations. The settlers were proud of their success and wanted people to see how beautiful their new land was.

Artists made pictures of the outdoors to show how people were changing the countryside. Artists also made pictures showing how the countryside looked before people changed it. This kind of art is called landscape*.

Instructions

1. Look carefully at the landscape pictures that go with this lesson. Pick out one picture and practice trying to remember everything that is in it.

2. Test your visual memory. You can do this in two ways. One is to list everything you see in the picture. The other is to make a drawing of the picture to show everything that you remember. Because this is an art

* *The meaning of this word is in the Glossary. (232-236)*

lesson, you are to do the drawing. Write the list first if you think it will help you.

3. Try not to look at the picture again until you are finished. Then look carefully at it. When you think you have seen all the parts you missed, add them to your work. You may have to look at the real picture more than once. But if you practice making drawings like this, your memory will get better.

American Artist, Unknown, "The Plantation"

The Metropolitan Museum of Art, Gift of Edgar William and Bernice Chrysler Garbisch, 1963

Edward Hicks, "The Residence of David Twining, 1787"

Colonial Williamsburg Foundation, Abby Aldrich Rockefeller Folk Art Collection, Williamsburg, Virginia

Lesson Objectives
UNDERSTANDING ART (Conceptual)
  Learn that early American artists made landscape pictures to show their homes and the countryside. (C)
MAKING ART (Performance)
  Test your memory by drawing a picture without looking at it. (A)

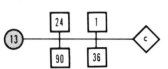
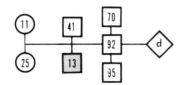
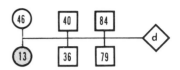
Lesson 13 — ARTISTS AND SCIENTISTS

Scientists learn about plants, animals, and rocks by studying their details. They measure, weigh, and describe their shape, color, and texture*. Artists do the same thing. They look closely at interesting things, then they draw them. These drawings help when an artist wants to add one of the objects to a picture.

This lesson will help you observe things more carefully to improve your pictures.

Instructions

1. Choose a simple object to draw. Think of something other than what is shown in the drawings that go with this lesson. Look carefully at the object and all of its parts.

2. Draw the object as well as you can. Begin with the outlines. Then shade the inside parts.

* *The meaning of this word is in the Glossary.* (232-236)

Try and add all the details that you see. Don't leave anything out.

3. The color pictures by Pieter Breughel (14A), Roger van der Weyden (17A), Hans Holbein (16), and Jan van Huysum (19) show how artists carefully study what they see.

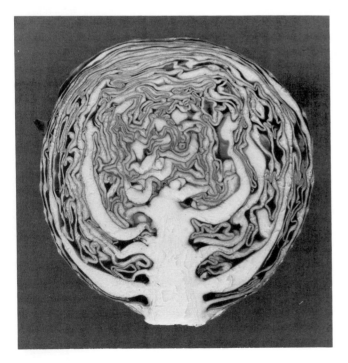

Jonell Folsom, ''Sweeney House''

Albrecht Dürer, ''A Dog''

Lesson Objectives

UNDERSTANDING ART (Conceptual)
   a. Explain the meaning of texture as the look or feel of a surface, such as rough, smooth, or silky. (B)
   b. Learn that artists as well as scientists study the things around them very carefully. (C)

MAKING ART (Performance)
   a. Draw in all the lines in a object. (A)
   b. Shade the light and dark parts of an object. (A)

Art Materials
A simple object to draw, such as a school desk, a chair, a water faucet, an old shoe, or a part of a car engine
Pencil and eraser
Drawing paper

Strand D   Strand F   Strand L

Lesson 14 — SONGS, POETRY, AND ART

Artists sometimes get ideas for their pictures from songs and poems. Sometimes they are asked to make pictures for books to show what is described in a poem or a song. The only way to get good ideas is to practice thinking up ideas.

Instructions

1. Read the poems on this page or find some in another book. Read them to yourself or say them aloud. Or you may like to sing the words of a song you like. A song is really a poem that is put to music. The poems or the songs should help you think of an interesting idea that could be made into a picture. The picture could show what the words say. Or it could be a design that doesn't show anything real, but seems to have the same feeling as the poem or song.

2. Paint a colorful picture or design of your best idea. Write the name of the song or poem on the front of the paper next to your name. This will be your title*. Write some of the words, too. This might help people see how your art and the words go together.

The meaning of this word is in the Glossary. (232-236)

Absolutes

black on white
crow in snow
  hunched
    wet lump
on brittle branch
remembering warmth
remembering corn
miserable
as life
is
black on white

i thank You God for most this amazing

i thank You God for most this amazing
day: for the leaping greenly spirits of trees
and a blue true dream of sky; and for everything
which is natural which is infinite which is yes

(i who have died am alive again today,
and this is the sun's birthday; this is the birth
day of life and of love and wings: and of the gay
great happening illimitably earth)

how should tasting touching hearing seeing
breathing any — lifted from the no
of all nothing — human merely being
doubt unimaginable You?

(now the ears of my ears awake and
now the eyes of my eyes are opened)

The Tomcat

At midnight in the alley
  A Tom-cat comes to wail,
And he changes the hate of a million years
  As he swings his snaky tail.

Malevolent, bony, brindled,
  Tiger and devil and bard,
His eyes are coals from the middle of Hell
  And his heart is black and hard.

He twists and crouches and capers
  And bares his curved sharp claws,
And he sings to the stars of the jungled nights
  Ere cities were, or laws.

Beast from a world primeval,
  He and his leaping clan,
When the blotched red moon leers over the roofs
  Give voice to their scorn of man.

He will lie on a rug to-morrow
  And lick his silky fur,
And veil the brute in his yellow eyes
  And play he's tame, and purr.

But at midnight in the alley
  He will crouch again and wail,
And beat the time for his demon's song
  With the swing of his demon's tail.

From THE AWAKENING AND OTHER POEMS by Don Marquis.
Reprinted by permission of Doubleday & Company, Inc.

Lesson Objectives
UNDERSTANDING ART (Conceptual)
    a. Learn that artists sometimes get ideas from poems
       and from songs. (C)
    b. Explain the word title in art as a name that describes
       what the art is about. (B)
MAKING ART (Performance)
      Paint a colorful picture or design. (F)
APPRECIATING ART (Affective)
      Show in art how a poem or song makes you feel. (D)

Art Materials
Paints
Pencil and eraser
White paper
Mixing tray
Scissors
Glue
Water, paper towels
Brushes

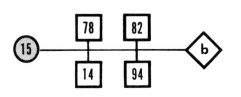
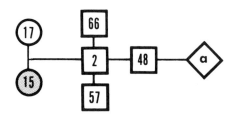
Lesson 15 — HARD-EDGE PAINTING

A popular way of painting today is with clean, sharp edges. It is called hard-edge* painting. Artists and advertising designers use it. It is especially good with geometric* designs that have many curves and straight lines. Hard-edge art also looks good with bright colors.

Instructions

1. Draw a simple design made of simple geometric shapes. Make it fill your paper. It could look like rainbows or neon signs or some other thing you have seen.

2. Mix some paint of medium thickness. Paint up to the lines in your design. Look at the illustration to see how to do it. If you

* The meaning of this word is in the Glossary. (232-236)

practice and are careful, you will soon be able to make a good hard-edge.

3. The pictures that go with this lesson may help you, but don't use the same ideas. The color pictures by Joan Miro (27A), Marc Chagall (27B), and Victor Vasarely (28B) all show art that has hard edges.

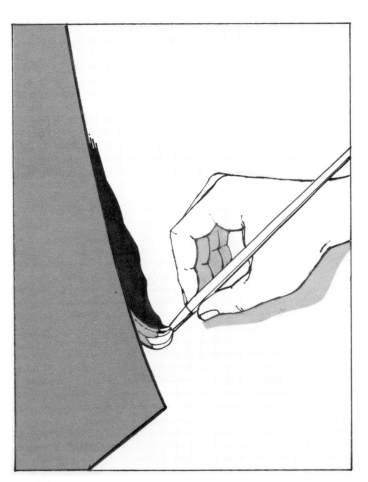

Frank Stella, "Lac Laronge IV"

The Toledo Museum of Art, Toledo, Ohio
Gift of Edward Drummond Libbey

Lesson Objectives
UNDERSTANDING ART (Conceptual)
  a. Learn how hard-edge painting is used. (C)
  b. Explain the meaning of geometric as having straight
     lines and simple curves. (B)
MAKING ART (Performance)
  a. Draw a geometric design. (F)
  b. Draw a design that reminds you of something you
     have seen before. (A)
  c. Practice carefully painting up to lines. (F)

Art Materials
White paper
Medium-sized brush
Scissors
Ruler
Set square
Tempera paint
Pencil and eraser
Paste and applicator
Compass
Water, paper towels

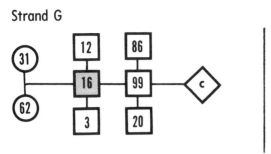
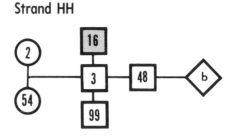
Lesson 16 — THE WILD, WILD WEST

Lots of movies and stories have been written about explorers, buffalo hunters, trappers, cowboys, Indians, rustlers, and the cavalry in the Wild West. Many artworks have been done describing the West, too. This art helped the people in the East and Midwest understand what the Wild West looked like. The pictures and sculptures of the West were also beautiful to look at.

Some famous Wild West artists were Charles Russell, Charles Wimer, Albert Bierstadt, and Frederic Remington. Wimer visited Indian camps, Bierstadt traveled with wagon trains and painted landscapes* of mountains. Remington and Russell painted pictures about cowboys, Indians, buffalo, and cattle on the wide open prairies. Remington also modeled sculptures of cowboys on horseback.

Instructions

1. Look at the pictures by these artists. Try and learn as much as you can from them. Notice how these artists painted. Get some ideas for your own picture from these artists.
* *The meaning of this word is in the Glossary. (232-236)*

2. Draw, then paint your own picture. Put into your picture the things you have learned by studying the Wild West artists. Remember, though, that the picture is to be your very own.

Albert Bierstadt, "Indians Near Fort Laramie"

Painted about 1858   Oil and paper mounted on cardboard. 13½ x 19½ in.
M. and M. Karolik Collection, 48.411   Courtesy Museum of Fine Arts, Boston

Frederic Remington, "The Emigrants"

The Museum of Fine Arts, Houston   The Hogg Brothers Collection

Lesson Objectives

UNDERSTANDING ART (Conceptual)

    Learn that Wimer, Bierstadt, Remington, and Russell were artists who showed how the Wild West looked. (C)

MAKING ART (Performance)

    Make your own picture of the Wild West. (F)

APPRECIATING ART (Affective)

    Choose ideas for a picture from artwork done by artists of the Wild West. (D)

Art Materials
Drawing paper
Paints
Brushes
Mixing trays
Water, paper towels
Pencil and eraser

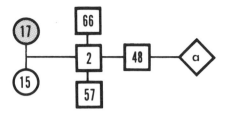
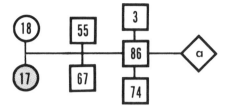
Lesson 17 — COVER-UP PAINTING

Have you ever thought of making a picture by taking part of it away? You often do this when you erase pencil marks. You get quite a different effect when you do it with paint. Here's how it is done.

Instructions

1. Take some rubber cement or some masking tape and cover up parts of a piece of paper. You can use both cement and tape if you like. The parts you cover up can be any parts of your paper. Or you can draw a picture first and cover some special parts of it. This picture should be mainly about tall swaying flowers, a tangled jungle, or an underwater forest of seaweed.

2. Paint your picture. Make your paint fairly thin. Let the paint dry. Slowly pull off some—not all—of the tape. To get the rubber cement off, gently rub it with your finger.

3. Now paint more parts of your picture. Decide how you want to paint the white parts of the picture that had been underneath the tape or cement.

4. When the paint is dry again, take off more of the cover-up tape and cement. You can also add fresh tape and cement in different places if you want to. Paint the picture some more.

5. When you think your picture is finished, let it dry completely. Be sure to take off all the rubber cement and masking tape.

Lesson Objectives

UNDERSTANDING ART (Conceptual)

   Learn that you can cover up, then take away parts of a picture to get special effects. (C)

MAKING ART (Performance)

   a. Paint with fairly thin paint. (E)
   b. Make a picture of many growing plants. (F)
   c. Add or take away rubber cement and masking tape. (E)

APPRECIATING ART (Affective)

   Decide on the parts of the picture where tape or cement is needed. (D)

Art Materials
Watercolors
Brushes
Rubber cement
Masking tape
White paper
Mixing trays
Water, paper towels

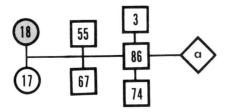

Lesson 18 — PAINTING FROM BACK TO FRONT

From a distance, hills, trees, and buildings seem to turn a whitish-purple or blue-gray color. This happens because dust, mist, or smoke changes the colors. Artists often show that things are far away by making their colors fade. They mix some white and purple or blue-gray with their colors.

Here is one way to show distance in a picture. You do it when you are painting with thin, watery paint.

Instructions

1. Draw an outdoor picture of a place you have been to. It could be hills and fields, a harbor, or rooftops in a big city. Or it could be a place you would like to go. This is called a landscape*. When you draw, do not press heavily. Leave out all details. Show some things close and some far away. The sky should be farthest away.

2. Use very thin, watery paint(†). First paint the parts farthest away. You don't have to paint too carefully. Use the proper colors, but mix them with some purple or blue-gray.

Let the paint dry. Notice that you can see through the paint. It is transparent*.

3. Now paint the parts that are next farthest away. The colors should have less purple or gray. They will be a little brighter and less watery. Let the paint dry.

4. Last of all, paint the things that are closest to you. Use bright-colored paint. It can be much thicker. Add as many details as you like. All the parts of the picture should be painted, even if the paint is very faint.

*The meaning of this word is in the Glossary. (232-236) † For an explanation turn to the How To Do It section. (237-250)

Shen Chou, ''Peach Blossom Valley''

Trustees of the British Museum

Joseph Mallord William Turner,
"Burning of the Houses of Parliament"

The Cleveland Museum of Art
Bequest of John L. Severance

Andrew Wyeth, "From Mount Kearsarge"

Indianapolis Museum of Art
Gift of Mrs. James W. Fesler

Lesson Objectives

UNDERSTANDING ART (Conceptual)
 a. Explain the meaning of landscape as a picture made of an outdoor scene. (B)
 b. Learn that colors fade in the distance. (C)
 c. Explain the meaning of transparent as being able to see through something. (B)

MAKING ART (Performance)
 a. Draw a landscape picture. (F)
 b. Paint the distant parts of a picture first, using pale colors mixed with purple or blue. (A)
 c. Paint the closest parts of a picture last, using bright colors. (A)
 d. Show paint in all parts of a picture. (A)

Art Materials
White paper
Brushes
Mixing tray
Paints
Water, paper towels
Pencil and eraser

67

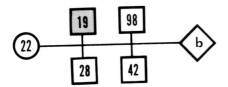

Lesson 19 — SCULPTURE WEAVING

Weaving* is used in so many things around us that we forget how important it is in everyday life. But weaving is also used to make things that are beautiful to look at without being useful. A piece of weaving can be just as good to hang on a wall as a painting would be.

In this lesson you will make some weaving that will be like a piece of sculpture.

Instructions

1. Find a branch that has fallen or has been cut from a tree. It should be between one and two feet long and have at least one place where it divides in two.

2. Wind yarn around the top and bottom parts of your branch to make the warp*. Fill in as much space as you think looks right. Tie the ends securely. The branch is now a loom*.

3. Weave over and under the warp threads with yarn, string, grass, or anything else you think will look good. These are your weft* threads. See how creative you can be with your weft threads.

4. Hang the finished weaving against the wall or hang it from the ceiling in the middle of the room.

* The meaning of this word is in the Glossary. (232-236)

68

Lesson Objectives

UNDERSTANDING ART (Conceptual)
a. Explain the meaning of weaving as the interlacing of yarn to make cloth. (B)
b. Explain the meaning of loom as a frame that is used for weaving. (B)
c. Learn how to weave using a warp and a weft. (C)

MAKING ART (Performance)
Make a weaving on a natural loom. (F)

APPRECIATING ART (Affective)
a. Choose interesting things to weave with. (D)
b. Decide on a creative way to weave the weft design. (D)

Art Materials
A branch
Yarn or string
Scissors
Any interesting material to work with

31 — 12 — 86
62 — 16 — 99 — c
3 — 20

76 — 20
29 — 70 — 92 — c
53

Lesson 20 — AMERICAN PAINTERS OF TODAY

Some of the greatest painters today are American. One of them is Edward Hopper. He paints pictures of places you see every day in towns and cities. Everything about his pictures is quiet and peaceful.

Another important American artist is Stuart Davis. His pictures are usually bright and colorful. They are made up of abstract* shapes that do not look real.

Jackson Pollock's paintings are done by dripping paint all over his pictures. His pictures are also abstract. But they look different from the paintings by Stuart Davis.

These three artists all work very differently. Still other American artists paint pictures that are even more different.

All artists try to do their work in their own way. So should you.

Instructions

1. Look carefully at the pictures that go with this lesson by Hopper and Davis. Also look at the color pictures by Jackson Pollock (26) and other American artists, such as Richard Lindner (28A), Peter Sedgley (13B), and Nancy Singleton (13A). Decide which way of painting you would like to use in your own

* *The meaning of this word is in the Glossary.* (232-236)

picture. You can take one idea from one artist and another idea from another artist.

2. Make your own picture. Paint it using some of the ideas from the pictures that are in this lesson and in the color section.

Stuart Davis, "Swing Landscape"

Courtesy of the Indiana University Art Museum

Edward Hopper, "Nighthawks"

Lesson Objectives

UNDERSTANDING ART (Conceptual)

Learn that Edward Hopper, Stuart Davis, and Jackson Pollock are important American painters. (C)

MAKING ART (Performance)

Paint a picture of your very own. (F)

APPRECIATING ART (Affective)

Choose ideas for your picture from the paintings that go with this lesson. (D)

Art Materials

White paper

Paints

Brushes

Mixing trays

Pencil and eraser

Water, paper towels

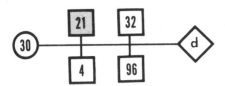

Lesson 21 — AMERICAN ARCHITECTS

American architects* are famous for designing beautiful buildings. Thomas Jefferson was the first of our great architects. He designed many buildings, including his own home called Monticello, two hundred years ago. Louis Sullivan worked in Chicago nearly a hundred years ago. He was the first architect to use steel to build tall skyscrapers*. Frank Lloyd Wright was designing very modern-looking houses over seventy years ago. Buckminster Fuller is still at work designing futuristic buildings called geodesic domes*.

Instructions

1. Collect boxes, sticks, cellophane, and other things to make a model of a building.

2. Think about the kind of building you would like to design. It can be a home, a sky-scraper, or a church. Look at the architects' designs that go with this lesson.

3. Design and make your own building. You might get some ideas from the pictures of architects' works that go with this lesson, or you might come up with some of your own.

4. Use paint, pencil, or crayon and draw in the small parts of the buildings.

* The meaning of this word is in the Glossary. (232-236)

Monticello, designed by Thomas Jefferson

Geodesic Dome, designed by Buckminster Fuller

Robie House, designed by Frank Lloyd Wright

Lesson Objectives

UNDERSTANDING ART (Conceptual)

a. Learn about American architecture by Thomas Jefferson, Louis Sullivan, Frank Lloyd Wright, and Buckminster Fuller. (C)

b. Explain the meaning of skyscraper as a very tall building that has a steel frame. (B)

c. Explain the meaning of geodesic dome as a lightweight dome built of triangular-shaped blocks. (B)

MAKING ART (Performance)

a. Put together a model of a building. (F)

b. Put in details on the model building. (A)

c. Attach objects so they will not come apart. (E)

APPRECIATING ART (Affective)

Choose ideas for a building from the work of great American architects. (D)

Art Materials

Choose only those that fit your idea for a building.

Cardboard boxes

Scissors

Glue and applicator

Soda straws, popsicle sticks, toothpicks, etc.

Construction paper

Pencil and eraser

Brushes and paints

Mixing trays

Crayons

Water, paper towels, etc.

Cellophane, aluminum foil, tissue paper

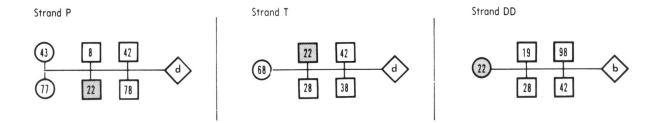

Strand P

Strand T

Strand DD

Lesson 22 — GEOMETRY WITH A NEEDLE

Pictures and designs can be made by using a needle and yarn*. This kind of art is called stitchery*. Stitchery can be a way of learning to be creative with straight lines.

Instructions

1. With a pencil, draw a square, a triangle, or any other geometric* shape between six and eight inches across. Draw it on very stiff paper or thin cardboard that is a color you like. Now cut(†) it out with scissors.

2. About an eighth of an inch from the edges of your shape, make a mark with pencil every quarter of an inch. Make small holes with a needle where your marks are. You might want to make some holes in the center of your shape.

3. Now thread your needle with wool, cotton, yarn, or silk. Choose a color that will look good with the color of your geometric shape. Tie a knot at the end of the yarn.

4. Start from the back of your shape. Push your needle through one of the holes. Pull the yarn through until you reach the knot. Now push the needle back into a hole on the front side of your shape. The yarn will lie across your shape to make a straight line.

5. Choose another hole and push the needle up through it. Repeat what you did before. Keep adding more lines like this. Change your yarn to make the design more interesting.

*The meaning of this word is in the Glossary. (232-236)   † For an explanation turn to the How To Do It section. (237-250)

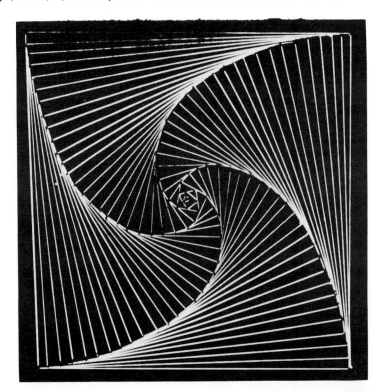

74

Sue Fuller, "String Composition #537"

Herron Museum of Art, Collection Alliance of the Indianapolis Museum of Art

Lesson Objectives
UNDERSTANDING ART (Conceptual)
   a. Learn how simple stitchery is done. (C)
   b. Explain the meaning of yarn as a strand-like material made of cotton, wool, or synthetic material. (B)

MAKING ART (Performance)
   a. Cut out a square, circle, or triangle in thin cardboard. (E)
   b. Mark out the edges every quarter of an inch and punch holes an eighth of an inch from the edges. (E)
   c. Make a stitchery design on a cardboard frame. (F)

APPRECIATING ART (Affective)
   Think of a creative way to divide up your shape. (D)

Art Materials
Needles with large eyes
Colored yarns of various kinds: cotton, wool, silk, nylon, etc.
Thick paper, thin cardboard, wire screen, or cloth
Ruler
Scissors
Pencils and erasers

Strand C

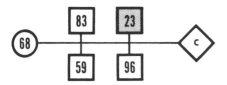

Lesson 23 — ART THAT BALANCES

Airplanes and balloons seem to float. Sculptors also make art that seems to float. The parts are all carefully balanced and they slowly twist and turn in the air currents. Artworks like this are called mobiles*. The artist who made this kind of art popular is Alexander Calder.

Instructions

1. Gather a collection of small, lightweight things. Tie pieces of thin thread to those that you think go well together.

2. Hang something from your collection from each end of a piece of stiff wire or a thin stick. Be sure the thread is tied tightly.

3. Tie a third piece of string to the middle of the stick. Hold this thread and let the stick dangle. Move the middle string until the two sides are hanging evenly. You have now finished one piece of your mobile.

4. Repeat steps two and three. You will then have finished two pieces of your mobile. Tie your two pieces onto another piece of stick or wire, one from each end. Find the balance point as you did before and tie on another piece of thread. You can stop now or keep adding to your mobile. Hang it from the ceiling and watch it gently twist and turn.

* The meaning of this word is in the Glossary. (232-236)

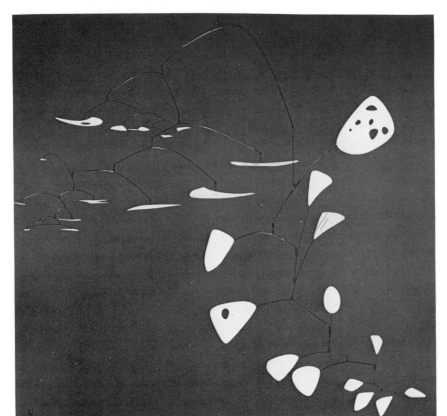

Alexander Calder, ''International Mobile''

The Museum of Fine Arts, Houston

Gift from D. and J. de Menil

In Memory of Marcel Schlumberger

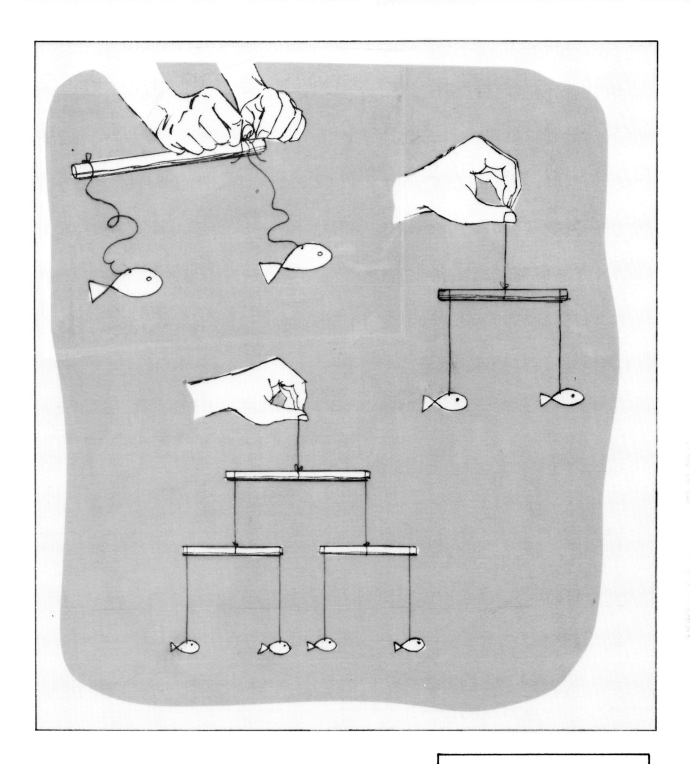

Lesson Objectives

UNDERSTANDING ART (Conceptual)
  a. Explain the meaning of mobile as a piece of hanging sculpture that is carefully balanced. (B)
  b. Learn that the art of making mobiles was made popular by Alexander Calder. (C)

MAKING ART (Performance)
  Build a mobile. (F)

APPRECIATING ART (Affective)
  Choose parts for a mobile that look good together. (D)

Art Materials
A collection of small, light-weight objects with small holes punched at one point: cardboard shapes, plastic or aluminum objects, etc.
Lengths of thread (4''-5'')
Lengths of stiff wire or straight sticks (8'')
Scissors, glue

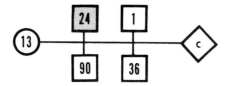

Lesson 24 — DETECTIVE WORK IN ART

You can see objects of different kinds every-where. Do you know what they really look like? The best way to test how well you know what something looks like is to draw it.

Even detectives and scientists can't see every-thing. They use magnifying glasses* and microscopes* to see some things. In this lesson you will be a detective.

Instructions

1. Make an outline drawing of a bicycle pedal, a roller skate, or a football helmet. You can choose some other interesting object to draw if you like. Just draw the main lines and draw them quite darkly by pressing on them with your pencil.

2. Next, look at the same object through a magnifying glass. Look closely.

The meaning of this word is in the Glossary. (232-236)

3. Draw in all the details you can see. You will now be able to see things clearly. Some things you cannot see at all without the magnifying glass to help you.

4. The drawing may not be quite as good as you would like it to be, but don't be unhappy. It takes lots of practice to be really good at anything.

Lesson Objectives
UNDERSTANDING ART (Conceptual)
    Learn that artists look closely at things. (C)
MAKING ART (Performance)
    a. Draw the outlines of an object. (F)
    b. Draw all the details of an object by looking through
       a magnifying glass. (A)

Art Materials
Objects to draw: door handle,
    lunch pail, stapler, flower
    vase, etc.
White paper
Pencil and eraser
Magnifying glass (shared)

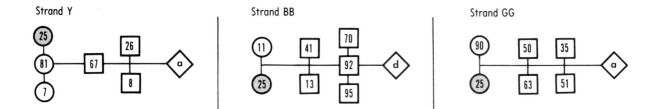

Strand Y

Strand BB

Strand GG

Lesson 25 — DOTS . . . DOTS . . . DOTS

A dot by itself doesn't move. It doesn't point anywhere. But lots of dots one after another make dotted lines. Dotted lines can point in different directions. Dotted lines can also make outlines of shapes. Pictures in newspapers are made from hundreds of dots that show light and dark shapes. They also show humps and hollows that are inside the shapes. This lesson is about using dots to draw.

Instructions

1. Make a large outline drawing in pencil of something you can see in the room. It can be a desk, a chair, a window, a vase, a piece of student sculpture, or anything at all. Be careful not to press heavily with your pencil.

2. Use pen and ink or a thin felt tip pen to finish your drawing. Draw only with the same sized dots. Put the dots close together to show darkness and farther apart for lightness. Show the background with dots, too.

Albright-Knox Art Gallery, Buffalo, New York, Consolidated Purchase Funds

Lesson Objectives

UNDERSTANDING ART (Conceptual)

Learn that dots can make lines and shapes and can be used to show shading. (C)

MAKING ART (Performance)

a. Make an outline of an object in pencil. (F)
b. Show the shading on an object with dots. (A)
c. Fill in all the background spaces in a picture with the right amount of dots. (A)

Art Materials
Pencils and erasers
Drawing paper
Pen and ink or thin felt tip pen

81

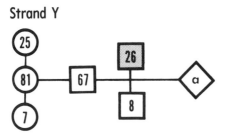

Lesson 26 — LILLIPUT

A famous English writer, Jonathan Swift, wrote Gulliver's Travels. In the book, Gulliver visited a land called Lilliput where the people were only six inches tall. Gulliver's Travels isn't a true story, but there is a real Lilliput all around us. It is so small that we can see it only if we magnify* it with a microscope*.

Artists and designers often use ideas in their work that come from things that are very small. Here is your chance to do that.

Instructions

1. Find some pictures of very small things that have been enlarged. The picture should be of something that is interesting to look at. It could be from your science book showing parts of a rock, a leaf, or an animal. Looking at something directly under a microscope would be even better than looking at a picture. What does your picture make you think of? A field of mushrooms? A heap of broken glass or some tangled roots?

* The meaning of this word is in the Glossary. (232-236)

2. When you have decided what the picture makes you think of, make a picture or a design that clearly shows what you see. You can use paint, crayons, pencils, or any other art materials you like. You can even mix different art materials together in a new way.

4. When your work is done, write on it somewhere what you saw in the enlarged picture. Be sure the work is your very own creation.

A seed magnified 70 times

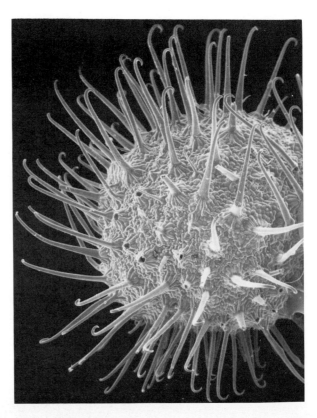

Insect larva and egg case magnified 1600 times

Human hair magnified 3,480 times

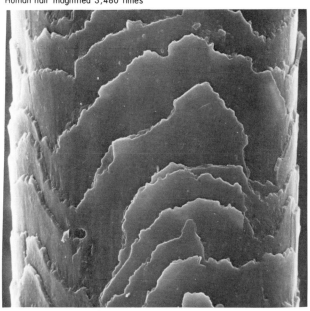

Glands on the bud of a plant magnified 725 times

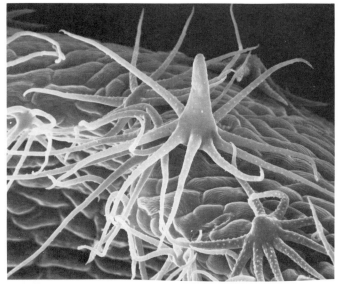

Lesson Objectives

UNDERSTANDING ART (Conceptual)

    a. Learn that artists get ideas by looking at very small things that can only be seen through a microscope. (C)

    b. Explain the meaning of magnify as making something look bigger. (B)

MAKING ART (Performance)

    a. Make a picture or design with any art materials. (F)

    b. Use ideas for work from things seen through a microscope. (A)

Art Materials

A photograph taken through a microscope

Any art materials: pencil and eraser, paints, crayons, pen and ink, felt tip pens, tissue paper and glue, etc.

Drawing paper

Microscope (optional)

Water, paper towels, etc.

Mixing trays

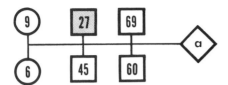

Lesson 27 — CHICAGO ARCHITECTURE

Chicago has been, and still is, the home of many great architects*. After the Great Chicago Fire in 1871, many brilliant architects helped to rebuild the city. In doing so they made Chicago the center of world architecture*. One of the most famous Chicago architects, Louis Sullivan, built the first tall building with a steel framework. These skyscrapers* are now a common sight in most cities. Many other architects learned from those in Chicago, and the city became famous for its innovative and well-designed buildings.

Instructions

1. Look at the pictures of Chicago skyscrapers. Notice how different they all look. Decide which building design looks best to you.

2. Make some drawings for a skyscraper design of your own. You can get ideas from the pictures of buildings you looked at.

* The meaning of this word is in the Glossary. (232-236)

3. Build a model for a very tall skyscraper. Erect the framework first. Make sure it will stand up easily. Then cover the framework with paper. You can draw on the paper before you stick it on to show things like windows and doors. Balconies, ledges, etc., can be stuck on later.

Carson, Pirie, Scott Building, designed by Louis Sullivan

Sears Tower

Marina Towers

John Hancock Center

Lesson Objectives

UNDERSTANDING ART (Conceptual)

a. Learn that Chicago is famous for its architects and the buildings they designed. (C)

b. Learn that Louis Sullivan was one of the greatest Chicago architects. (C)

MAKING ART (Performance)

a. Draw ideas for skyscraper designs. (F)

b. Build your own design of a model skyscraper. (F)

c. Add all the details which belong on your building. (A)

Art Materials

Long wooden sticks

Tongue depressors

Toothpicks

Paper

Glue and applicator

Pen and ink or pencil

Small objects for balconies, air conditioners, stairways, antennas, etc.

Strand T

Strand DD

Lesson 28 — CREATING WITH STITCHES

Can you imagine painting with a needle and thread? For hundreds of years artisans have done this when they made tapestries* and embroideries*. A popular art form today is stitchery*, which is making pictures and designs with needle and thread. After this lesson you will have your own stitchery.

Instructions

1. Use white chalk and draw a simple design on a piece of cloth.

2. Use the stitches that go with this lesson to fill in the design. Add any other kinds of stitches you know. You may want to practice the stitches before you begin your stitchery.

3. Show the big shapes first by outlining them with running or back stitches. Use satin or chain stitches to fill in the spaces. Try all of the stitches to find out what is best for you. You can add buttons and sequins* to make your stitchery look more interesting.

* The meaning of this word is in the Glossary. (232-236)

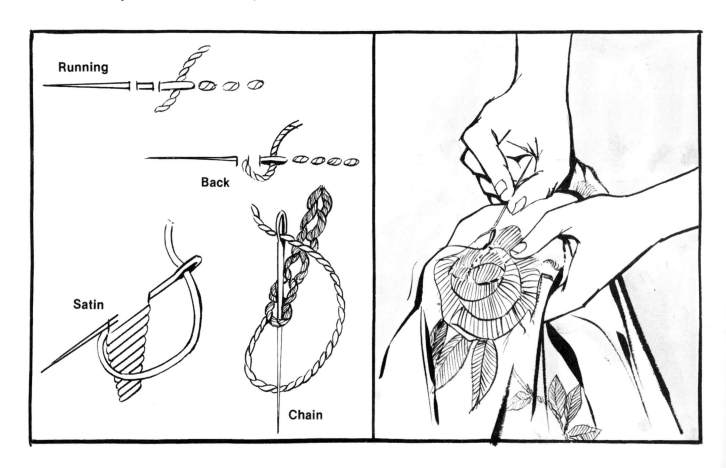

Leah Orr, "Catalyst"

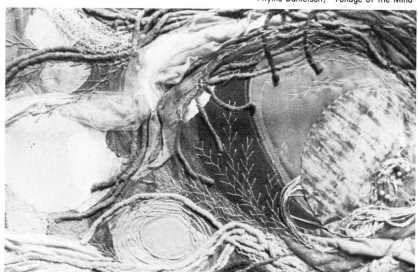

Phyllis Danielson, "Foliage of the Mind"

Lesson Objectives

UNDERSTANDING ART (Conceptual)
  a. Explain the meaning of tapestry as a large picture that is woven in cloth and hung on a wall. (B)
  b. Explain the meaning of embroidery as designs and pictures made with needle and thread. (B)
  c. Learn that art can be made with creative stitchery. (C)
  d. Explain the meaning of sequin as a small shiny metal circle that can be stitched to cloth. (B)

MAKING ART (Performance)
  a. Make running or back stitches. (E)
  b. Make satin or chain stitches. (E)
  c. Make a piece of stitchery. (F)

APPRECIATING ART (Affective)
  Decide how to improve your stitchery with buttons and sequins. (D)

Art Materials
Darning or tapestry needles with large eyes
Chalk
Background cloth: burlap, linen, poplin, etc.
Yarn materials: wool yarn, embroidery silk, raffia, twine, etc.
Scissors
Buttons, sequins, etc.

87

Strand Q

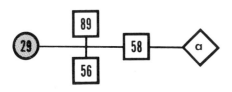

Strand S

Lesson 29 — GUESS WHAT IT WAS

Sometimes when you look at a picture it is difficult to decide what it is about. Often the picture doesn't look like anything at all. Some artists never think of anything real to begin with. Others start with something real and then change it to something abstract*. Here is one way of being creative and making an abstract picture.

Instructions

1. Find a picture you like that you think you could draw. Make a fairly small pencil drawing of this picture.

2. Put the picture out of sight until the end of the lesson. Make another drawing with thick crayon of the same scene on a larger sheet of paper. Look only at your small drawing for help. Hold your crayon in the hand you do not usually use for drawing.

* *The meaning of this word is in the Glossary. (232-236)*

3. Put the small drawing away. Turn the large one upside down and fasten it to the wall farthest from you. Draw the scene again with a brush and black paint with the hand you usually use for drawing.

4. Add other lines, shapes, and colors until the painting looks finished. Take out the first picture and the three drawings and see how each one has changed.

Paul Gauguin, "The Yellow Christ"

Albright-Knox Art Gallery, Buffalo, New York, Consolidated Purchase Funds

Lesson Objectives
UNDERSTANDING ART (Conceptual)
  a. Learn that some artists start with real things and change them. (C)
  b. Explain the meaning of abstract in art as using pieces of things instead of making them look real. (B)
MAKING ART (Performance)
  Make three different drawings of the same picture using three different art materials. (A)
APPRECIATING ART (Affective)
  a. Decide on the best way to finish a picture. (D)
  b. Notice how the three drawings are different. (A)

Art Materials
Pencil and eraser
Drawing paper
A picture to draw
Large brush
Paints, crayons
Mixing tray
Water, paper towels, etc.

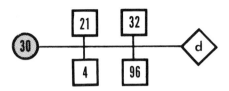

Lesson 30 — BUILDINGS IN THE MIDDLE AGES

During the Middle Ages (400 - 1500 A.D.) churches, cathedrals*, castles, and manor houses were the most important buildings. They had beautiful features including large towers, steeples*, colorful stained glass windows, and arches*. The style of the arches gradually changed throughout the years from rounded to pointed.

Instructions

1. Look at a picture of a house, castle, or cathedral that was built in the Middle Ages.

2. Draw the building in the picture with pencil. Draw it as carefully as you can.

* The meaning of this word is in the Glossary. (232-236)

If you cannot draw all the shapes exactly right, don't be unhappy. It takes a lot of practice to learn to draw things to look real. All you should try to do in this lesson is to put in all the parts of the building you can.

Bodiam Castle, England

Cathedral of Cologne, Germany

Little Mireton Hall, England

Lesson Objectives

UNDERSTANDING ART (Conceptual)

    a. Learn that church buildings were the most important ones in the Middle Ages. (C)

    b. Learn that the style of arches changed from rounded to pointed. (C)

    c. Learn that windows in important buildings were sometimes decorated with colored glass. (C)

MAKING ART (Performance)

    Draw a church or castle that was built in the Middle Ages. (F)

Art Materials
Drawing paper
Pencil and eraser
Clear photograph of a church or cathedral built in the Middle Ages

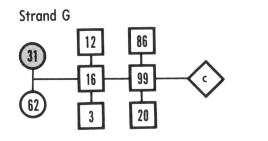
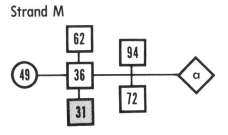

Lesson 31 — MICHELANGELO

Michelangelo was a great Italian artist who lived over four hundred years ago in Rome and Florence. He designed buildings, carved sculptures, and painted pictures. One of his best sculptures is called "Moses" and is in Rome.

He was one of the architects* of St. Peter's Church in Rome, the largest Christian church in the world. One of his greatest paintings fills the entire ceiling of the Sistine Chapel, a church in Rome.

Instructions

1. Look at these artworks by Michelangelo. What do the people look like? What kind of people are they? Why do you think he made his people the way they are? Did he have some special reason for making them that way?

* *The meaning of this word is in the Glossary. (232-236)*

2. After you have looked carefully at the artworks and thought about the questions, you should be ready to answer them. Write your answers on a sheet of paper and show them to your teacher.

Michelangelo, Sistine Chapel Ceiling Detail

Vatican Museum Photographic Archives

Michelangelo, ''Moses'', Church of St. Peter's, Vatican City

Vatican Museum Photographic Archives

Michelangelo, ''Studies for the Libyan Sibyl''

The Metropolitan Museum of Art
Purchase, 1924, Joseph Pulitzer Bequest.

Lesson Objectives
UNDERSTANDING ART (Conceptual)
    a. Learn who Michelangelo was and the kinds of art
       he created. (C)
    b. Write down answers to questions about Michelangelo's
       buildings, paintings, and sculptures. (D)

Art Materials
Writing paper
Pencil and eraser

93

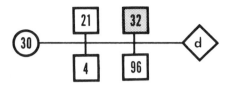

Lesson 32 — MODERN ARCHITECTS

Good architects* all over the world are designing buildings to fit the needs of the people who will use them. Architects no longer try to copy buildings designed hundreds of years ago. A Swiss architect, Le Corbusier, has designed heavy, solid-looking buildings with interiors that look almost like caves. An Italian, Pier Luigi Nervi, has designed buildings that have smooth, curving shapes. The Danish architect, Joern Utzon, designed the opera house in Sydney, Australia. He used jagged shapes one on top of the other.

Instructions

1. Look at the pictures with this lesson. Think about the buildings in your town. Are any of the buildings in your town like the buildings in the pictures? How are they different? What do most of the buildings look like in your community? What are they used for?

2. Write down the answers to those questions. You can show what kinds of buildings are in your town with your own drawings, or you can include pictures if that will help you answer the questions more easily.

* *The meaning of this word is in the Glossary. (232-236)*

Opera House, Sydney, Australia, designed by Joern Utzon

Roman Catholic Cathedral of Tokyo, designed by Kenzo Tange

David S. Ingalls Hockey Rink, Yale University, designed by Eero Saarineu

Lesson Objectives
UNDERSTANDING ART (Conceptual)
a. Learn about the kinds of buildings architects are designing today. (C)
b. Learn that some important architects are Le Corbusier, Pier Luigi Nervi, and Joern Utzon. (C)
c. Answer questions about buildings in your town. (D)

Art Materials
Sheet of paper
Pencil and eraser

95

Strand W

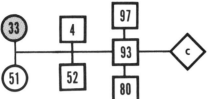

Strand EE

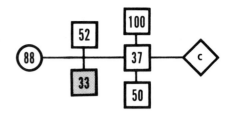

Lesson 33 — HAND SCULPTURE

Artists generally use two ways of making sculpture*. One is by putting pieces together, the other is by cutting pieces away, or carving*. In this lesson you will carve something to fit your hands. Your hand will tell you when the artwork is done. You don't need to make it look like anything real.

Instructions

1. You will need a solid block of wax, soap, plaster(†), or anything else you can carve easily. Cut into the block so that you make the sculpture fit the shape of your hand comfortably. Be careful not to cut away too much.

2. Make the surface pleasing to touch. It should look good as well. Some parts can be smooth and others can be rough. You can put a special pattern on it. Finish the surface so that it feels good to touch.

*The meaning of this word is in the Glossary. (232-236)   † For an explanation turn to the How To Do It section. (237-250)

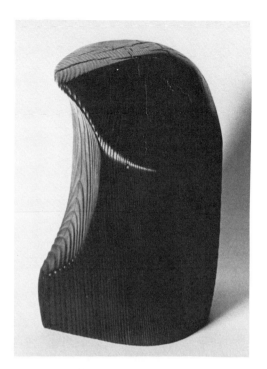

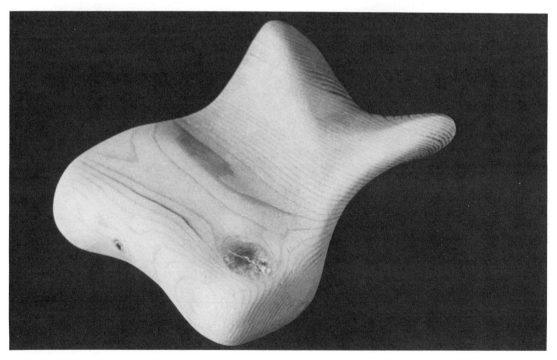

Lesson Objectives
UNDERSTANDING ART (Conceptual)
    Learn about two ways to make sculpture. (C)
MAKING ART (Performance)
    Carve a piece of hand sculpture. (E)
APPRECIATING ART (Affective)
  a. Decide when your sculpture fits your hand. (D)
  b. Decide if your sculpture is pleasing to look at. (D)
  c. Decide when the surface of your sculpture is good to look at and to touch. (D)

Art Materials
Block for carving: paraffin wax, soap, plaster, clay, styrofoam, soft wood
Cutting tool: knife, rasp*
Sandpaper
Polish, etc., for final finish

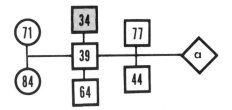

Lesson 34 — SLICE, TWIST, AND STRETCH

It's fun to change things to see what happens. You can twist, squash, or stretch them. Artists are always thinking of new ways to change things. That's what this lesson is all about.

Instructions

1. Cut out(†) a picture of a person's face. It should be at least as big as your hand. Cut the face into slices of different thicknesses. Cut it across or up and down.

2. Arrange the slices in order on a piece of paper. Play with the pieces to change the face. The pieces mustn't overlap but they may be moved in any other way you like. Make sure it still looks like a face when you're finished.

3. When you have found a good arrangement of the slices, glue(†) them in place. The face should now look different than it did. It is now distorted*.

4. Now draw the distorted face on another sheet of paper. Pretend the spaces between the slices are not there. If it is hard to draw the face freehand*, trace(†) it. Write a title for the face on your drawing.

*The meaning of this word is in the Glossary. (232-236)   † For an explanation turn to the How To Do It section. (237-250)

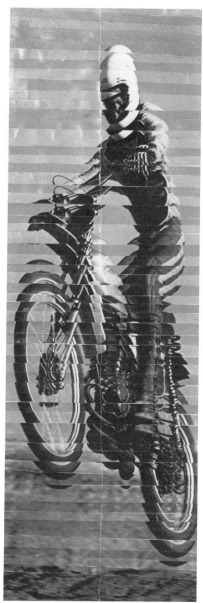

Lesson Objectives

UNDERSTANDING ART (Conceptual)
  a. Learn that creative artists are always trying out new ideas. (C)
  b. Learn about one way of making a distortion. (C)

MAKING ART (Performance)
  a. Make a distorted face design by spacing out the parts. (F)
  b. Cut paper with scissors. (E)
  c. Stick paper together firmly. (E)
  d. Make a drawing of a distorted face. (F)

APPRECIATING ART (Affective)
  Write in a title that describes the distorted face. (D)

Art Materials
Drawing paper
Pencil and eraser
Picture of a face
Scissors
Glue and applicator

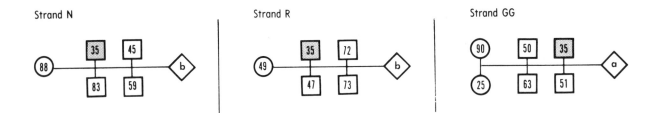

Strand N

Strand R

Strand GG

Lesson 35 — SKELETON SCULPTURE

Tall, thin sculpture* made of clay* or plaster* will not stand up by itself. It needs something inside it to hold it up. People have bones to hold them up. The thick wire or metal pipe that sculptors put inside their work is like a skeleton. This is called an armature*. For smaller things you can use a wadded ball of newspaper. Chicken wire is also good to help hold sculpture up. This lesson is about making sculpture that needs an armature.

Instructions

1. Think about how people look when they are running, dancing, or throwing a ball. Bend a piece of wire so that it looks like a person doing one of those things. This is your armature; it should be about ten inches high. Tape or twist other pieces of wire together to make the armature strong. Nail or staple the armature to a piece of wood so that it is able to stand up by itself.

2. Put clay(†) or plaster(†) on the armature until it is the proper thickness for the parts of the body. Model the figure so it looks real. Make all the main parts of the body look right.

The meaning of this word is in the Glossary. (232-236) † For an explanation turn to the How To Do It section. (237-250)

Frederic Remington, "Bronco Buster"

Courtesy of The Art Institute of Chicago

Alberto Giacometti, "Man Pointing", Third View

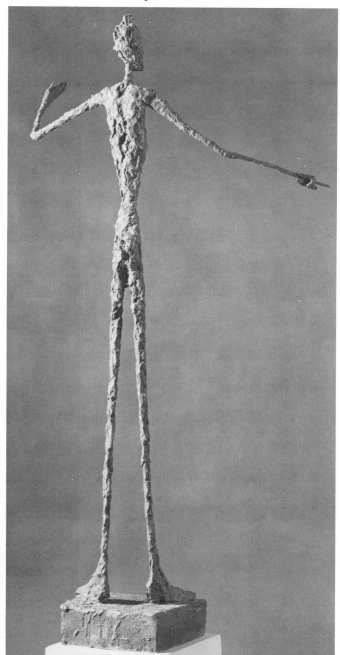

The Tate Gallery, London

Ernest Heinrich Barlach, "The Avenger"

The Tate Gallery, London

Lesson Objectives
UNDERSTANDING ART (Conceptual)
    Learn why sculptors use armatures. (C)
MAKING ART (Performance)
  a. Bend wire to make an armature. (E)
  b. Model a figure over the armature. (F)
APPRECIATING ART (Affective)
    Decide when your sculptured figure looks right and
    shows plenty of action. (A)

Art Materials
Thick, soft wire (24"-36")
Masking tape, string, wire
Stapler and staples or hammer
    and nails
Pieces of wood (base)
Oil or plastic-based clay
Newspaper (to cover desk)
Pliers
Plaster of paris

101

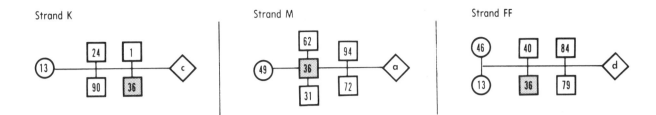

Strand K

Strand M

Strand FF

Lesson 36 — THE RENAISSANCE

During the Renaissance (1300-1600), there were exciting changes in art. European artists began to make their work look more real. Sculptors created statues with accurate details that looked like real people. Painters began to use scenes from everyday life. Some colors were dark and mysterious; others were bright and lifelike. Even the architecture* changed. Buildings fit the needs of the people and walls and pillars* were filled with decoration.

Instructions

1. Look at the pictures that go with this lesson. Look at the ways the artists made their lines and shapes.

2. Draw a picture that shows your family or friends at a place you know. The important thing to remember is to draw your picture in the way that these artists did their pictures.
* The meaning of this word is in the Glossary. (232-236)

3. Now paint your picture. Get your ideas from the ways that the artists painted their pictures. Use the same kinds of colors they did.

4. The color pictures by Leonardo da Vinci (15A), El Greco (14B), and Titian (15B) show the kinds of colors these artists used.

Titian, ''Bacchus and Ariadne''

Reproduced by courtesy of the Trustees, The National Gallery, London

102

Leonardo da Vinci, "Virgin of the Rocks"

Lesson Objectives

UNDERSTANDING ART (Conceptual)

Learn about the Renaissance and the changes in art during that period. (C)

MAKING ART (Performance)

Draw and paint a picture in the way art was done during the Renaissance. (F)

APPRECIATING ART (Affective)

Choose ways of drawing and painting for your own pictures that show the way art was done during the Renaissance. (D)

Art Materials
White paper
Paints, brushes
Mixing trays
Pencil and eraser
Water, paper towels

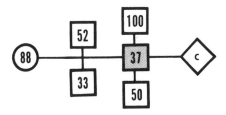

Lesson 37 — CREATIVITY WITH BEADS

People wear strings of beads to make themselves look better. Sometimes people think the beads have a magical meaning. They may protect a person from being ill or being attacked by evil spirits. Beads may also show how important or rich a person is. In this lesson you will string beads together to show how creative you can be.

Instructions

1. You can make beads easily out of papier-mâché or clay(†) that has been fired*. Beads can also be made out of wood, glass, and stone. They can be made out of anything that has a small hole in it. Small parts of clocks and other machines often have holes in them. You can make holes in sea shells, beans, nuts, and other natural things. Make a collection of things you could use for beads.

Be as original* as you can when you make your collection.

2. Experiment with different ways of stringing beads together. You might be able to get some ideas from the pictures with this lesson. Make a string of beads that shows how creative you are. Wear your beads after this lesson has been completed.

* The meaning of this word is in the Glossary. (232-236)   † For an explanation turn to the How To Do It section. (237-250)

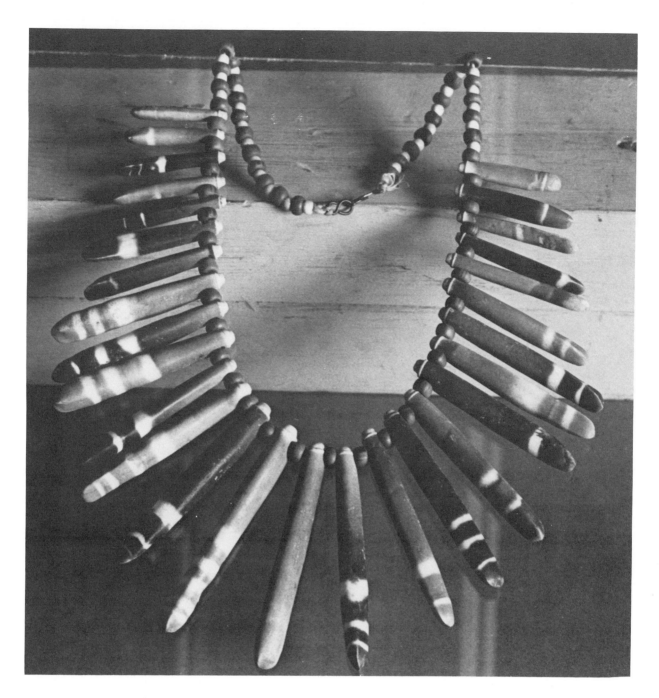

Lesson Objectives

UNDERSTANDING ART (Conceptual)
  a. Learn that people wear beads to decorate themselves and sometimes for magical reasons. (C)
  b. Learn that beads can be made from many things. (C)

MAKING ART (Performance)
  a. Make a collection of things for beads. (A)
  b. Make a string of beads. (F)

APPRECIATING ART (Affective)
  a. Decide which beads in your collection are the most interesting to use. (D)
  b. Decide which way of stringing beads together is the most creative. (D)

Art Materials
Thin string, thread, or nylon
  fishing line
Scissors
Papier-mâché or clay
Hammer and nail
Collection of beads or objects
  that could be used as beads

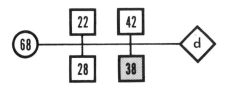

Lesson 38 — SOFT SCULPTURE

Most sculpture* feels hard when it is finished. It might be made of wood, metal, stone, plaster, or clay. Another kind of sculpture is soft. It is made from pieces of cloth that are sewn into interesting shapes and filled to make them solid. This kind of art is called soft sculpture. Look at the pictures that go with this lesson to see what soft sculpture looks like.

Instructions

1. Draw a large, simple shape on a piece of paper. It could be one of the initials in your name, a simple animal shape, a moon, a heart, or just a shape you like.

2. Place two pieces of cloth the same size together. Draw your shape on the cloth to almost fill the size of the cloth. Cut out(†) the cloth shape with scissors, one half inch bigger than the shape you drew. Keep both pieces of cloth together when you cut.

3. Thread a needle. Sew the shapes together exactly on the line you drew. When you have sewn nearly all the way around, turn the shape inside out. The ragged edges will be inside.

4. Fill your shape with cotton, scraps of old cloth, or strips of soft paper. When the shape is as fat as you want it, tuck in the edges and close the opening.

5. If your shape looks nice as it is, then your sculpture is finished. You might want to decorate it with pieces of cloth, buttons and sequins*, or a design with paint, ink, or felt tip markers.

*The meaning of this word is in the Glossary. (232-236)   † For an explanation turn to the How To Do It section. (237-250)

Detail of soft sculpture by Barbara Kensler

Chris Carpenter, ''Beautiful Dreamer''

Phyllis Danielson, ''Time Rushes By''

Lesson Objectives

UNDERSTANDING ART (Conceptual)
    Learn that sculpture can be soft. (C)
MAKING ART (Performance)
    a. Thread a needle. (E)
    b. Stitch two pieces of cloth together. (E)
    c. Decorate your soft sculpture. (F)
APPRECIATING ART (Affective)
    Decide how to decorate your soft sculpture. (D)

Art Materials
Drawing paper
Needle and thread
Pencil and eraser
Two pieces of cloth (12'' square or larger)
Scraps for filling

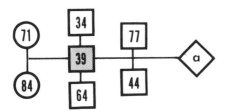

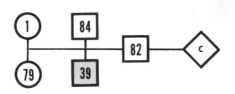

Lesson 39 — CARICATURES

Some artists are famous for their beautiful pictures of people; others are famous for pictures that poke fun at people. These pictures exaggerate a person's features. A person who is tall and skinny will look as thin as a piece of string. Newspapers have these pictures, or caricatures*, in them. A caricature is a special kind of distortion*.

Instructions

1. Find some photographs of famous people such as athletes, movie stars, or politicians. Look for photographs of people who would be good subjects for caricatures. Do they have some feature that you could exaggerate?

The meaning of this word is in the Glossary. (232-236)

2. Look carefully at the photograph you chose. Draw your own caricature of that person. Change some of the features so they are very distorted. There are some pictures of caricatures with this lesson that might help you.

Lesson Objectives

UNDERSTANDING ART (Conceptual)

    a. Explain the meaning of caricature as a picture of a person with some of his or her features exaggerated. (B)

    b. Explain the meaning of distortion as changing the way something looks to make it more interesting. (B)

MAKING ART (Performance)

    a. Draw a caricature of a famous person. (F)

    b. Show some part of a caricature as a distortion. (A)

Art Materials
Photographs of famous people
Pencil and eraser
Drawing paper

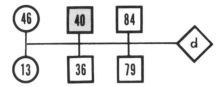

Lesson 40 — THE ART OF NEW ORLEANS

The people who first came to the lands around the Gulf of Mexico were the Spanish and the French. The French built a city near the mouth of the Mississippi River; they named it New Orleans after a city in France. The ideas for the art and architecture* of New Orleans came from France. The city was different from any other city in the New World. Some of the old buildings are still standing in New Orleans and the countryside around it. This lesson is to help you learn what these old buildings look like.

Instructions

1. Look at the pictures of old buildings that go with this lesson. Decide which one looks the most interesting to you. Which one would you most like to remember?

2. Copy the picture you like best. If you aren't very good at copying, trace(†) it.

3. Now draw the picture again; don't trace it this time. If you forget something, look at the picture again. Write the name of the place on the front of your paper. You have finished this lesson when you can draw the building without looking at a picture of it.

* *The meaning of this word is in the Glossary. (232-236)*   † *For an explanation turn to the How To Do It section. (237-250)*

The Shadows on the Teche

Gallier House

St. Louis Cathedral

Lesson Objectives

UNDERSTANDING ART (Conceptual)

Learn that the ideas for art and architecture in New Orleans came from France. (C)

MAKING ART (Performance)

a. Copy a picture of a building as well as you can. (A)

b. Practice drawing that building until you can do it from memory. (A)

Art Materials
Pencil and eraser
Drawing paper

111

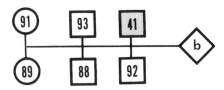

Lesson 41 — I KNOW THAT PLACE!

You know the places near your home, the service stations, supermarkets, stores, and schools. Yet how well do you really know them? Can you describe how they look? Could you draw or paint any of them? Here is your chance to test your visual memory.

Instructions

1. Think of all the places in your neighborhood. Pick out one you think you know well. Write the name of the place at the top of a sheet of drawing paper. Then write down all the things you can remember about it.

2. Turn your paper over and draw the place you described. Make the drawing fill the whole paper. Look at your description to help you remember everything about it.

3. Color your drawing with paint, crayon, or felt tip marker. Go to the place you drew after school and see if you remembered everything about it. Add more details to your drawing later if you forgot anything.

4. The color pictures by Pierre Renoir (22B), Claude Monet (22A), Vincent Van Gogh (23), and Alfred Sisley (24B) all show places the artists knew very well.

Richard Estes, "Drugstore"

Courtesy of The Art Institute of Chicago

Lesson Objectives

UNDERSTANDING ART (Conceptual)

Learn that remembering the way things look is important. (C)

MAKING ART (Performance)

a. Write a list of everything you remember about a place you know. (A)

b. Draw a place you know well from memory. (F)

c. Decide how accurate your drawing is by going to look at the real place. (A)

Art Materials
White paper
Pencil and eraser
Paints, crayons, felt tip markers
Brushes
Mixing tray
Water, paper towels

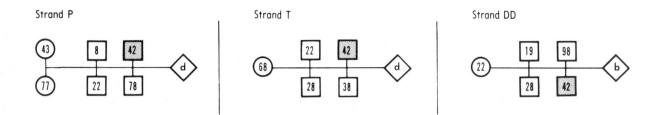

Strand P

Strand T

Strand DD

Lesson 42 — PICTURES IN CLOTH

Pictures made of cloth and hung on walls are called wall hangings*. One way of making the picture for a wall hanging is by stitching pieces of cloth together. This is called appliqué*.

Instructions

1. Smooth out a piece of cloth for the background of your appliqué wall hanging. Make it a shape, size, and color you like. Think of interesting shapes that have something to do with the seasons of the year. Draw an idea for your wall hanging on paper first.

2. Choose different pieces of cloth that would look good on the background. Cut these pieces into the shapes you made on your drawing. Arrange them into a picture or design that you like. Then draw around the shapes with chalk so you know where they go.

3. Thread a needle. Stitch the pieces onto the background. Look at Lesson 28 for some ideas about stitching. When you're finished, staple or tack your wall hanging onto a straight stick and hang it on the wall. Look at the pictures that go with this lesson for ideas. The color picture of art by Richard Lindner (28A) shows an appliqué wall hanging.

* The meaning of this word is in the Glossary. (232-236)

Margaret M. Somerville, Stitchery: Cockerel Motif

Victoria and Albert Museum, Crown Copyright

114

Lesson Objectives

UNDERSTANDING ART (Conceptual)
   a. Learn that one kind of picture is called a wall hanging and is made of cloth. (C)
   b. Learn that appliqué is made by stitching pieces of cloth onto a background.(C)

MAKING ART (Performance)
   a. Make an appliqué wall hanging. (F)
   b. Stitch cloth pieces onto background material. (E)

Art Materials
Large piece of cloth
Small pieces of cloth
Needle and thread (different colors)
String
Paper, scissors
Straight stick, stapler
Pencil and eraser

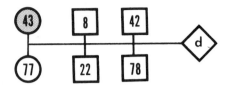

Lesson 43 — GEOMETRICS

In school you probably use rulers, compasses*, set squares*, protractors*, and even T squares* and templates*. Usually you use those drawing instruments in geometry or industrial arts for making exact shapes and measurements. These kind of instruments are just as good for making creative pictures and designs as they are for other subjects.

Instructions

1. Find a picture that you think is interesting. It should not have many geometric* shapes or straight lines in it. It can be a photograph of a famous painting or a picture from a magazine. Choose one with lots of things to see.

2. Use the picture as a guide for your art. Make a drawing of the picture. Make every mark with a drawing instrument(†). Nothing is to be done freehand*.

3. When you have made the shapes that are in the picture with drawing instruments, add anything you think would make your drawing look better. Remember to use only drawing instruments for all your shapes.

4. The color pictures by Joan Miró (27A), Marc Chagall (27B), and Victor Vasarely (28B) show the kind of art you will do in this lesson.

*The meaning of this word is in the Glossary. (232-236)   † For an explanation turn to the How To Do It section. (237-250)

Thomas Hart Benton, "July Hay"

The Metropolitan Museum of Art, George A. Hearn Fund, 1943.

Lesson Objectives

UNDERSTANDING ART (Conceptual)

Learn that drawing instruments can be used for making creative art. (C)

MAKING ART (Performance)

a. Make a picture using only drawing instruments. (F)

b. Base your drawing on a picture by someone else. (A)

APPRECIATING ART (Affective)

a. Choose a picture you like. (D)

b. Decide when to change the shapes to geometrics. (D)

Art Materials

Pencil and eraser

Ruler, compass, set square, protractor, T square, template, etc.

Drawing paper

Drawing board and thumb tacks (with T square)

117

Strand A

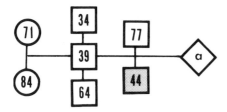

Lesson 44 — PETS AND THEIR PEOPLE

Have you ever watched people and their pets together? Did you ever see any pets that looked like their owners? A man might look like his bulldog. A woman's hair might look like her poodle's. Imagine what a picture would look like if it showed different kinds of pets and their owners. Would the pets look more like humans or the humans more like pets?

Instructions

1. Look at pictures of animals and try to think of what their owners' faces would look like. Pets can be from anywhere in the world. They can be cats and dogs, or they can be unusual pets like crocodiles or spiders.

2. Draw a big picture of a pet with its owner. They should look like each other. Use the pictures of people and animals by Albrecht Dürer (18A) and Richard Lindner (28A) to help you.

Lesson Objectives

MAKING ART (Performance)
 a. Make drawings of pets and their owners that look like each other. (F)
 b. Show many different pairs of pets and owners. (A)

Art Materials
Drawing paper
Pencil and eraser
Book and magazine pictures
 of pets and people

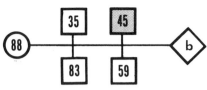
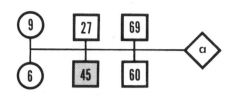
Lesson 45 — THE GOLDEN GATES OF SAN FRANCISCO

San Francisco is the home of many artists and designers. The most famous piece of design is not a painting or a building, but a bridge. It hangs on steel cables and stretches across the entrance to San Francisco Bay. Bridges that hang like that are called suspension bridges. There are famous bridges of all kinds all over the world. How would you like to design and build a bridge of your own?

Instructions

1. Engineers design bridges. They have to make their bridges strong as well as nice looking. Look at pictures of famous bridges; find the kind of design you would like to make.

2. Draw your own bridge design, then build it. It can be made of toothpicks, pieces of cardboard, or clay. You can use wire and string and anything else to make it look right.

Sydney Harbor Bridge, Sydney, Australia

120

Golden Gate Bridge, San Francisco, California

Tower Bridge, London, England

Lesson Objectives
UNDERSTANDING ART (Conceptual)
    Learn that bridges can be works of art. (C)
MAKING ART (Performance)
    a. Draw some designs for a bridge you will build. (F)
    b. Build a model of a bridge you designed. (F)
    c. Attach materials together strongly. (E)

Art Materials
Paper and pencil
Drawing paper
Glue and applicator
Materials for model bridge:
    toothpicks, cardboard, clay,
    popsicle sticks, string, wire,
    rope, etc.
Scissors

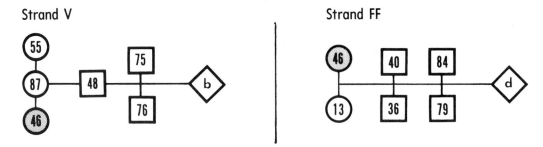

Strand V

Strand FF

Lesson 46 — BEING LIKE A CAMERA'S EYE

Cameras take pictures that show things looking real. It may be difficult to draw things to look real, but we can learn a lot about how things look from photographs. They can also help us learn to draw better.

Instructions

1. Find a fairly large photograph in a magazine of a normal-looking view of a simple, square-shaped object, like furniture inside a room or the outside of a building. A corner of the room or building should be near the center of the picture.

2. Cut the photograph out and glue it to a sheet of white paper. The sheet of paper should be about four inches bigger at the top and at the bottom. It should be about twelve inches bigger at each side. You may have to tape two or three sheets of paper together to make a piece that is big enough.

3. Find all the lines in the picture that are horizontal* or level. Use a ruler and draw pencil lines exactly on top of all these lines. Begin drawing the ends of the lines

*The meaning of this word is in the Glossary. (232-236)

that are closest in the picture. Keep drawing each line until your pencil goes off the photograph and onto the white paper. Keep drawing until each line goes off the edge of the white paper.

4. Notice that most of the lines in the photograph showing things that are horizontal seem to slope up or down. But the vertical lines on the objects do not change. Notice that most of these sloping lines come together on the white paper at each side of the picture. Cameras see these sloping lines, and so do we.

5. Now test yourself to see what you have learned. Make a freehand* drawing of the same photograph but do not show the lines you drew. Try to make your drawing look real.

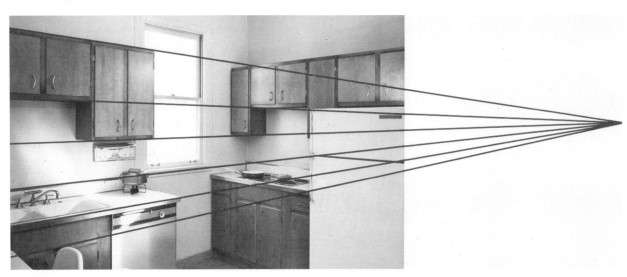

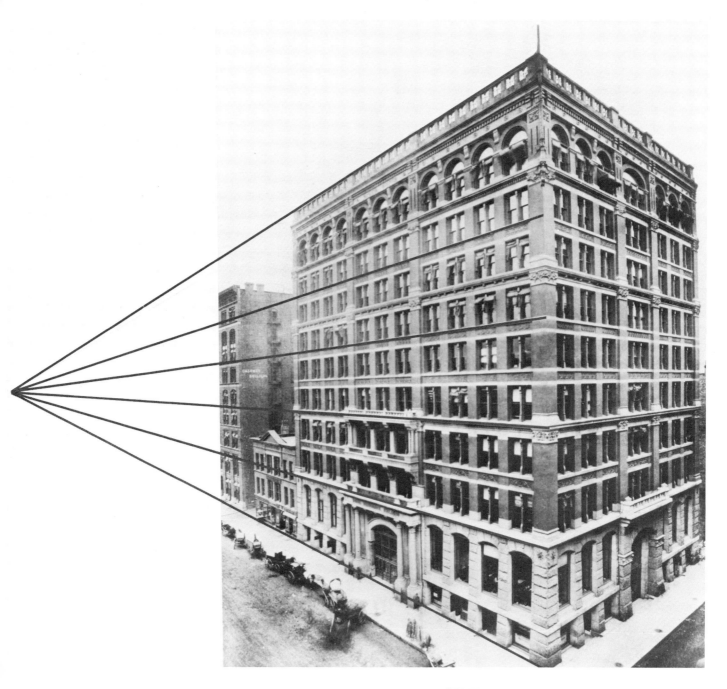

Lesson Objectives

UNDERSTANDING ART (Conceptual)
 a. Learn that photographs can help people draw more realistically. (C)
 b. Learn that horizontal lines seem to slope toward one another as they get farther away. (C)
 c. Learn that vertical lines in pictures usually remain vertical. (C)

MAKING ART (Performance)
 a. Make a freehand drawing of part of a room or a building that looks realistic. (F)
 b. Show horizontal lines in a picture sloping together. (A)
 c. Show vertical lines in a picture remaining vertical. (A)

Art Materials
Magazine photograph of a room or building
Scissors
Glue and applicator
Drawing paper
Tape
Ruler
Pencil and eraser

123

Strand B

Strand R

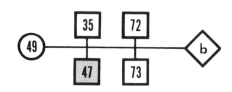

Lesson 47 — STIFFENED SCULPTURE

If someone breaks an arm, the doctor wraps it in bandages soaked in plaster. The plaster makes the bandages stiffen when dry, in order to hold the arm in one position while it mends. In the same way, everything made of fiberglass is made of a soft blanket of tiny glass threads.

Then a special glue, called resin*, is added. This glue sinks into the blanket; when it sets, the blanket becomes as hard as a rock. Fiberglass is used to make chairs, boats, car bodies, and many other things. This lesson is about turning soft cloth into stiff sculptures*.

Instructions

1. Mix up some white glue with a little water. You can also use laundry starch or plaster of paris(†). Soak a piece of cloth in the gluey water. Then squeeze most of the glue out and hang the cloth up to dry a little.

2. When the cloth begins to stiffen, make it into the shape of a person, animal, or design. If you use strips of cloth, you can place them over a person's face and make a mold

that is a perfect copy. Put facial tissue over the face before using the gluey strips.

3. When the sculpture is done, put the cloth in a safe place to dry. Then you can paint some thick glue over it to make it stronger.

4. When that layer of glue is dry, you can decorate the sculpture with paint or magic markers to make it more interesting.

The meaning of this word is in the Glossary. (232-236) † *For an explanation turn to the How To Do It section. (237-250)*

A mask by Brian Lillie

Alice Shaddle, "Illinois Landscape, 1974"

Lesson Objectives

UNDERSTANDING ART (Conceptual)

Learn that artists and designers soak cloth in plaster and different kinds of glue to make hard, solid-looking artwork. (B)

MAKING ART (Performance)

a. Make a piece of sculpture out of cloth soaked in plaster or glue. (F)

b. Decorate the surface of a piece of sculpture. (F)

APPRECIATING ART (Affective)

a. Decide on an interesting shape for your sculpture. (D)

b. Decide how to best decorate your sculpture. (D)

Art Materials

White glue

If you want to use laundry starch, mix it thicker than the package directions.

Plaster of paris

Piece of cloth

Scissors

Paints, magic markers, etc.

125

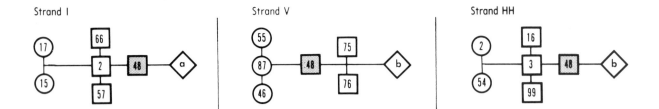

Strand I   Strand V   Strand HH

Lesson 48 — TRACE YOUR IDEAS

When artists create new things, they often do it quickly. Tracing paper is the one way to develop new ideas without spending a lot of time making drawings. A good idea is the most important thing you need. This lesson helps you learn to trace creatively.

Instructions

1. Put some slides in a projector. Focus the pictures clearly on a wall. Look at each slide and decide which things look good. You might pick trees from one slide; a house might come from another slide. Plan how to use these different parts together to make one picture.

2. Tape the corners of your paper to the wall and trace(†) over the picture from the slide as it shows on your paper. Put the part you like just where you want it on the paper. Do this for each slide that has something you like and can use in your picture.

3. If the images on the wall are too big, move the projector closer to the wall and check the focus again. When the drawing is done, paint your picture.

† For an explanation turn to the How To Do It section. (237-250)

Lesson Objectives
UNDERSTANDING ART (Conceptual)
   a. Learn that good ideas are important in art. (C)
   b. Learn that slides can help you draw. (C)
MAKING ART (Performance)
   a. Focus a slide on a wall. (E)
   b. Trace a shape as it shows on a wall. (E)
   c. Put together a picture made of parts of different pictures. (F)
APPRECIATING ART (Affective)
   Choose parts of slides to make a new picture. (D)

Art Materials
Slides and projector
Drawing paper
Pencil and eraser
Mixing tray
Paints and brushes
Water, paper towels, etc.
Cellophane tape

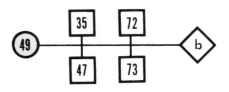

Strand M

Strand R

Lesson 49 — HUMAN MEASUREMENTS

People are different shapes and sizes, but a tall person is usually long in all parts of his or her body and a short person is usually short in all parts. Artists know what people's measurements usually are. This lesson will help you draw human measurements correctly.

Instructions

1. Read all these measurements. Because all the parts are measured against other parts, they are called proportions* or ratios*.

  a. The height of a person's head goes into his total height about seven times.

  b. A hand is as big as a face from the chin to where the hair begins.

  c. The length of a foot equals the height of a head.

  d. The arm and hand equal half the height from the shoulders to the ground.

  e. The hips come halfway between the top of the head and the ground.

  f. The upper and lower arm are equal.

* *The meaning of this word is in the Glossary. (232-236)*

  g. The knee comes halfway up the leg.

  h. The arm and hand stretch halfway down the leg to the knee.

2. Now draw someone in your class. Put in all the lines and shadows. Keep checking all the measurements as you work to make the drawing look right. The drawing may not be the best art you have ever done, but be sure the proportions are right.

3. The color pictures of people by Titian (15B) and Georges Seurat (21A) may help you draw human measurements properly.

Lesson Objectives

UNDERSTANDING ART (Conceptual)

    a. Explain the meaning of proportion in art as the size measurement of one thing compared with the size measurement of another thing. We can also use the word ratio. (B)

    b. Learn that the proportions of human bodies are all about the same. (C)

MAKING ART (Performance)

        Draw a person with all the body parts in proportion. (A)

Art Materials
Drawing paper
Pencil and eraser

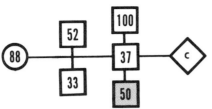
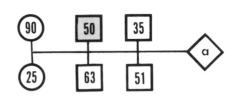
Lesson 50 — PRINTMAKING WITH LINOLEUM BLOCKS

Printmaking is a kind of art. It is different from painting and drawing because artists can make many prints from one idea. Newspapers, books, and posters are all printed. Thousands are printed on machines as fast as possible.

Each print by an artist is done carefully one by one. One way of making prints is by using blocks* made of linoleum, wood, or anything else that has been cut especially to make a design.

Instructions

1. Find a simple picture of an animal or a plant; or you could make your own design.

2. Paint the smooth top of a piece of linoleum white. Let the paint dry. Place some carbon paper with the inked side down on the linoleum. Place your picture on top. Draw the lines of your picture. The carbon paper will transfer* the design onto the white linoleum.

3. Cut the linoleum with the special cutters; always cut away from yourself. Follow the lines you traced to help you cut. Cut the spaces inside the lines so they are interesting.

The meaning of this word is in the Glossary. (232-236)

4. Spread some printing ink on something flat with a special roller called a brayer*. If you don't have a brayer, make a hard pad of cloth and spread the ink evenly by dabbing with the pad. Now roll the ink evenly on the linoleum block with a brayer, or dab it on with a pad.

5. Lay a piece of thin white paper on the block. Rub it gently with the round bottom of a spoon. Peel the paper away from the block; there is your print. Hang it up to dry.

6. The color pictures by Hokusai (18B) and Hiroshige (20A) are prints by famous artists.

Japanese student

Mexican student

130

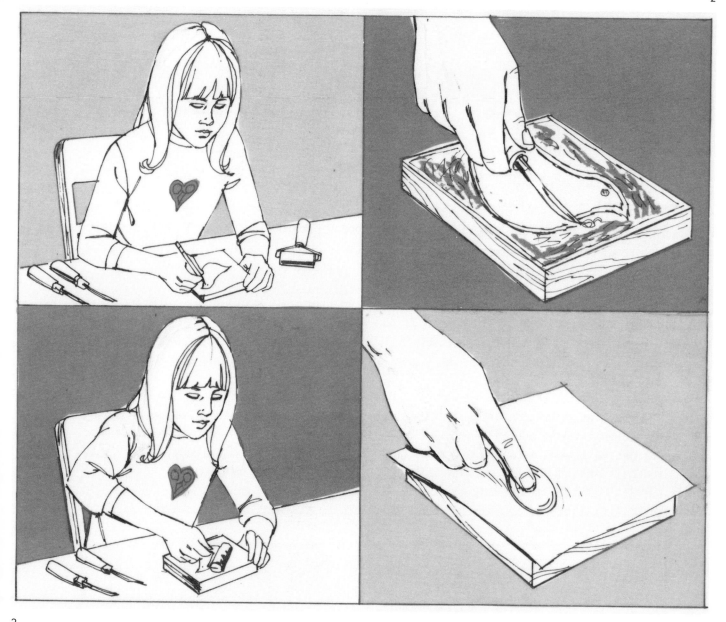

1

2

3

4

Lesson Objectives

UNDERSTANDING ART (Conceptual)

   a. Explain the meaning of a block used for printing as something solid that has a design cut into it. (B)

   b. Learn that thousands of newspapers and books are printed very quickly. (C)

MAKING ART (Performance)

   a. Choose a design or make up your own. (A)

   b. Transfer a design to a linoleum block. (E)

   c. Cut a design with linoleum cutters. (E)

   d. Print with linoleum block. (E)

Art Materials

Thick linoleum — 2″ x 3″
Linoleum cutting tools
Printer's ink (water soluble)
Thin paper for printing
Drawing paper for designing
Carbon paper
Water, paper towels
Plenty of newspaper
Pencil and eraser
Brayer or hard cloth pad
Kitchen spoon
Sheet of thick glass or a
   plastic dinner tray

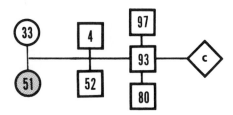
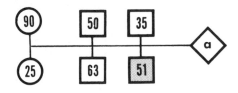
Lesson 51 — CARVING

Changing something in any way is a form of creativity*. You can change a solid block of wood into small sculptures of animals, people, or plants by carving*. Some sculptors carve in stone. In this lesson you are going to do some carving.

Instructions

1. Get a block of something fairly soft to carve. The list of art materials may give you some ideas.

2. Make a rough drawing of the shape you want to carve on the side of the block. It can look real or unreal; it can be a person, an animal, or anything else you like. Try to make the shape fill as much of the block as possible. Cut your shape out a little at a time.

3. Now draw your shape on the top of the block as it would appear if you were looking down at it. Cut these parts away slowly and carefully. You are now ready to put in all the details of your carving.

The meaning of this word is in the Glossary. (232-236)

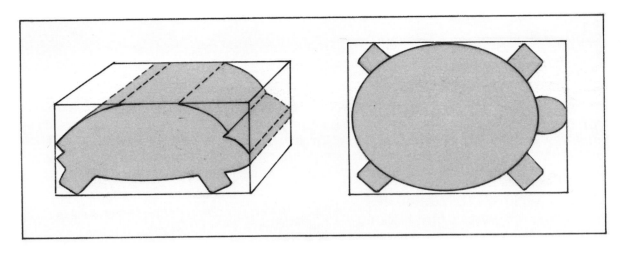

Alaskan Eskimo Art

Courtesy of the Indiana University Museum

132

Fang Tribe, "Figure on an Inigki Stand"

Felix Eboigbe, "Standing Figure"

Courtesy of the Indiana University Art Museum

Sculptor Felix Eboigbe at work in his studio.

Lesson Objectives

UNDERSTANDING ART (Conceptual)

    a. Explain the meaning of creativity as making something with imagination. (B)

    b. Explain the meaning of carving as making sculpture by cutting away unwanted parts. (B)

MAKING ART (Performance)

    a. Cut a shape from a block of something soft enough to carve. (E)

    b. Carve the side view of the shape. (A)

    c. Carve the top view of the shape. (A)

    d. Carve the details of the shape. (A)

Art Materials

A block to carve: soft wood (white pine), paraffin wax, firebrick, fairly hard clay, plaster, etc.

Sharp knife

Newspaper for scraps

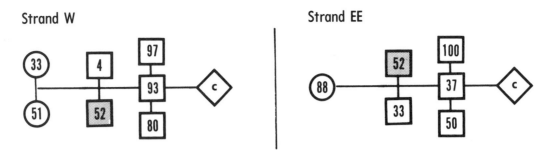

Strand W

Strand EE

Lesson 52 — ANCIENT ART OF MEXICO

Great art was being made in Mexico thousands of years ago. The people built large cities. They made giant carvings in stone and modeled smaller things in clay. They covered their sculptures with gold, feathers, sea shells, and precious stones. Unfortunately, only a few of these great artworks remain today.

Artists often borrow ideas for their work. In this lesson you will borrow ideas from ancient Mexico.

Instructions

1. Look carefully at the pictures of ancient Mexican art. Think about them and the way they look. Then ask yourself these questions. How do they make you feel? Do they seem to be telling you something?

2. Now make a painting or clay (†) sculpture of your own that has ideas and feelings in it like those in Mexican art. Use the same kinds of subjects, designs, and decorations you saw in the Mexican art.

† For an explanation turn to the How To Do It section. (237-250)

Atlantis — Tula

Tlatilco

Teotihuacan

Mexico, Archaic Colima culture, Dancing warrior holding spindle —
object in front, half fanlike — lower part of headdress missing

Courtesy of The Art Institute of Chicago

Precolumbian Teotihuacan, "Rain Priest"

Courtesy of The Art Institute of Chicago

Lesson Objectives

UNDERSTANDING ART (Conceptual)

    a. Learn about the great art of ancient Mexico. (C)

    b. Learn that artists often get good ideas from art
done by other people. (C)

MAKING ART (Performance)

    Make an artwork that shows ideas from ancient
Mexican art. (F)

APPRECIATING ART (Affective)

    Show feelings in your art like those in ancient
Mexican art. (D)

Art Materials
Paints, brushes, etc.
Clay
Newspaper
Drawing paper
Water, paper towels, etc.
Kitchen knife
Pencil and eraser

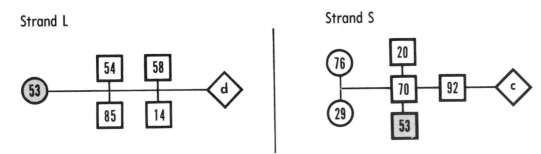

Strand L

Strand S

Lesson 53 — THE FATHERS OF MODERN ART

Sometimes art is done in the same style for hundreds of years; then something seems to happen. A few artists begin to work in ways that are very different and gradually the styles change. Three avant-garde* artists who introduced new styles to the world of art in the nineteenth century are Vincent Van Gogh, Paul Gauguin, and Paul Cezanne. Each one of them painted very differently.

Van Gogh painted his best pictures in the sunny south of France. His pictures were done in lines of thick, bright colors. Cezanne also worked in the south of France. The things in his pictures seem to be cut out of something solid; his colors are soft and quiet. Gauguin went to the tropical Pacific island of Tahiti and painted the hot, bright colors and lovely, brown-skinned people he found there.

Instructions

1. Look at the pictures painted by Van Gogh, Gauguin, and Cezanne. The best ones to look at are in the color pages. There is one by Vincent Van Gogh (23), Paul Gauguin (24A), and Paul Cezanne (21B). Choose one you like.

2. Draw your own picture or copy what you see in one of these pictures.

3. Paint (†) or color your drawing in the way that one of these artists did. You can decide to draw your own picture and paint it in the way that one of the artists painted. You can draw a picture by one of them and then paint it in the way one of the others would have, or you may draw and paint a picture by just one of the artists.

* The meaning of this word is in the Glossary. (232-236)   † For an explanation turn to the How To Do It section. (237-250)

Vincent Van Gogh, "View at Auvers"

The Tate Gallery, London

Paul Cezanne, "Mont Sainte-Victoire"

The Metropolitan Museum of Art, Bequest of Mrs. H. O. Havemeyer, 1929
The H. O. Havemeyer Collection

Paul Gauguin, "The Yellow Christ"

Albright-Knox Art Gallery, Buffalo, New York
Consolidated Purchase Funds

Lesson Objectives

UNDERSTANDING ART (Conceptual)
  a. Learn that three artists changed the way pictures are painted. Their names are Vincent Van Gogh, Paul Gauguin, and Paul Cezanne. (C)
  b. Learn what pictures by Van Gogh, Gauguin, and Cezanne look like. (A)

MAKING ART (Performance)
  Paint a picture like these artists did. (F)

APPRECIATING ART (Affective)
  Decide which of these artists' styles you want to use in your art. (D)

Art Materials
Drawing paper
Pencil and eraser
Paints
Brushes
Water, paper towels, etc.

137

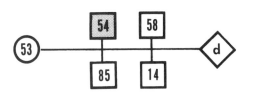
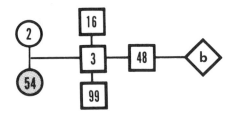
Lesson 54 — BIRD'S-EYE VIEW

As birds fly along, they see roofs, treetops, and people's heads. They look down on the things we must look up at to see. This is called a bird's-eye view*. People can get a bird's-eye view from the top of a tall ladder, a window in a skyscraper, or a plane.

Instructions

1. Imagine that you are a bird flying just above the rooftops and trees near where you live. What do you think you would see? How would things look different?

* *The meaning of this word is in the Glossary. (232-236)*

2. Draw a picture of someplace near where you live. Make the horizon near the top of your picture. Draw the scene the way a bird would see it when flying above it.

Finnish student

Camille Pissarro, "Place du Theatre Francais, Pluie, 1898"

The Minneapolis Institute of Arts

Lesson Objectives
UNDERSTANDING ART (Conceptual)
    Explain the meaning of bird's-eye view as looking down on things the way birds see them. (B)
MAKING ART (Performance)
  a. Draw a place near where you live. (F)
  b. Make a bird's-eye view drawing. (F)

Art Materials
Drawing paper
Pencil and eraser

139

Strand V

Strand CC

Lesson 55 — SHADOWS

Have you ever seen your shadow stretch out in front of you when the sun is behind you? Shadows are always on the sides of things that are away from the light. Shadows can be important parts of pictures, and artists use them to put special feelings into their work. The best shadows are made by light coming from one place near to the ground such as a lamp, a campfire, or a car's headlights.

Instructions

1. Imagine you are looking toward one source of light. It could be an open doorway or the moon at night. It could be car headlights or a flash of lightning.

2. Make a picture that shows light coming toward you. Put people and any other things you like in the way of the light. These shapes will be all dark. They are silhouettes*. Their shadows will stretch toward you. The shadows can be ghostly and scary or funny.

3. The light may also shine on other things in the picture. It will brighten one side and darken the other. Shadows help fill spaces in your artwork to make it look better.

* The meaning of this word is in the Glossary. (232-236)

Rembrandt, "A Scholar in a Lofty Room"

Charles Burchfield, "Ice Glare". 1933

Watercolor on paper. 30 3/4 x 24 3/4 inches
Collection of Whitney Museum of American Art

Lesson Objectives

UNDERSTANDING ART (Conceptual)
   a. Learn that long shadows are made when the light comes from near ground level. (C)
   b. Learn that shadows help fill the spaces in pictures to make them look better. (C)
   c. Explain the meaning of silhouette as the outline of something with no details inside. (B)

MAKING ART (Performance)
   Paint a picture showing silhouettes and long shadows coming toward you. (E)

APPRECIATING ART (Affective)
   Decide how shadows can make your picture look more interesting. (D)

Art Materials
Drawing paper
Paints
Brushes
Mixing tray
Water, paper towels
Pencil and eraser

Lesson 56 — GREAT MEXICAN ARTISTS

After the Mexican Revolution of 1910, many artists told the story of the revolution through large paintings on the walls of buildings called murals*. Four of these Mexican mural artists were José Clemente Orozco, Rufino Tamayo, David Siqueiros, and Diego Rivera. Their works all look different, but they are all very big and bold. While parts of their pictures are realistic, some parts have been changed through distortion*.

Instructions

1. Look at the pictures by Orozco, Siqueiros, Rivera, and Tamayo.

2. Draw an idea for a large mural on a big piece of paper. Make the design from your own imagination. You might tell a story through your mural if you'd like. Do it in the style of one of the Mexican artists. If you can, enlarge your design and put it on a wall to make a real mural.

* The meaning of this word is in the Glossary. (232-236)

David Alfaro Siqueiros, "The People for the University, the University for the People"

José Clemente Orozco, "Zapatistas", 1931.   Oil on canvas, 45" x 55"

Collection, The Museum of Modern Art, New York. Given anonymously

Rufino Tamayo, "Animals", 1941.   Oil on canvas, 30 1/8" x 40"

Collection, The Museum of Modern Art, New York. Inter-American Fund

Fresco, 7' 9 3/4" x 6' 2"

Collection, The Museum of Modern Art, New York. Abby Aldrich Rockefeller Fund

Lesson Objectives

UNDERSTANDING ART (Conceptual)

    a. Explain the meaning of mural as a painting done on a wall. (B)

    b. Learn that four Mexican mural painters are Siqueiros, Rivera, Orozco, and Tamayo. (C)

    c. Explain the meaning of distortion as changing the way something looks to make it more interesting. (B)

MAKING ART (Performance)

    a. Draw an idea for a mural. (F)

    b. Use ideas for mural art by Siqueiros, Orozco, Rivera, and Tamayo. (A)

APPRECIATING ART (Affective)

    Decide which artist has a style you like. (D)

Art Materials
Drawing paper
Pencil and eraser

143

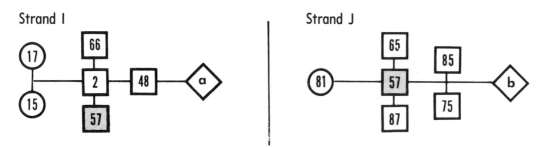

Strand I

Strand J

Lesson 57 — NIGHT AND DAY

Everything looks different at night. Sometimes you cannot even recognize a place at night, although you know it during the day. If you arrive at a strange place when it is dark, you might be very surprised in the morning. After you have seen a place at night and during the day, you forget how different it can look. This lesson is to help you remember these differences. It will also help you think of ways to make your pictures more interesting.

Instructions

1. Draw a picture of a street in a city or a town. It can be the community you live in or a place you made up. Put in the cars and people, as well as the trees and buildings.

2. Trace(†) your drawing. Make the tracing on another piece of paper that is the same size.

3. Turn one drawing into a daylight picture with paints, crayons, oil pastels, or felt tip markers. Make it a bright, sunny day.

4. Turn the other drawing into a nighttime picture. Remember that nighttime darkness is more like blue than black.

† For an explanation turn to the How To Do It section. (237-250)

M. C. Escher, ''Day and Night'', 1938

National Gallery of Art, Washington, D. C., Gift of C.V.S. Roosevelt

Lesson Objectives

UNDERSTANDING ART (Conceptual)

Remember how places look different at night and during the day. (A)

MAKING ART (Performance)

a. Make two pictures of the same place, one at night and one during the day. (F)

b. Make a tracing of a drawing. (E)

APPRECIATING ART (Affective)

Decide what kinds of differences there are in how something looks during the day and at night. (A)

Art Materials

Pencil and eraser

Paints, crayons, felt tip markers, oil pastels, etc.

Newspaper

Water, paper towels, etc.

Drawing paper

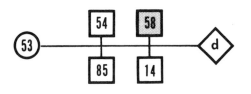

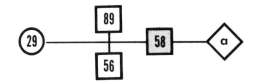

Strand L   Strand Q

Lesson 58 — CATASTROPHE

Artists have drawn and painted many sudden disasters, or catastrophes. Natural catastrophes are things like earthquakes and tornadoes. Man-made catastrophes might be bombings or fires. These artists don't usually try to make their pictures realistic, because photographers can do that. Instead they try to make us feel the horror of the catastrophe, as well as the helplessness and fear people feel when things go suddenly and terribly wrong.

Instructions

1. Decide on the kind of catastrophe you are going to tell about in your artwork. The pictures that go with this lesson might help you. Also look at the color picture by J. M. W. Turner (25B) that shows a terrible fire.

2. Think about the colors that would be best for your subject. Also plan what things and shapes will be shown in your artwork. You might want to practice some of them.

3. Draw your picture when you are sure of everything that will be in it. Remember that the picture is to tell about the feeling of a catastrophe. Use any art materials or any combination of materials you like.

146

Pablo Picasso, "Guernica". (1937, May - early June).   Oil on canvas, 11' 5½" x 25' 5¾".

On extended loan to The Museum of Modern Art, New York, from the artist.

Australian student

Lesson Objectives

UNDERSTANDING ART (Conceptual)
- a. Learn that artists use catastrophes as subjects for their art. (C)
- b. Learn that artists sometimes mix different art materials together in their work. (C)

MAKING ART (Performance)

Make a picture of a catastrophe. (F)

APPRECIATING ART (Affective)

Decide what feelings to show in your picture. (D)

Art Materials
Drawing paper
Paints, crayons, felt tip markers, oil pastels, etc.
Pencil and eraser

147

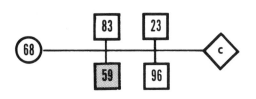
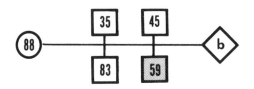
Lesson 59 — SKELETON ART

Buildings have skeletons, much like people do, except theirs are made of steel. The steel beams are covered with concrete, plastic, or glass to complete the building. If the building is covered with glass, the skeleton will still be visible. Bridges aren't covered by anything, so you can always see their skeletons. You can learn a lot about something by learning about what holds it up. In this lesson you will build some skeleton art of your own.

Instructions

1. Draw something you would like to build. It might be a bridge, a building, a spaceship, or just an unusual shape that you have created from your imagination.

2. Glue(†) soda straws, popsicle sticks, or toothpicks together to build the skeleton of what you have designed. Use only one of these things to build your design, although you may shorten some of them if you need to.

3. When your skeleton is finished, cover it with cellophane or plastic wrap so you can see the skeleton underneath.

† For an explanation turn to the How To Do It section. (237-250)

Geodesic Dome, Montreal

Watts Towers, Los Angeles

Eiffel Tower, Paris

Lesson Objectives

UNDERSTANDING ART (Conceptual)

Learn that both people and buildings have a strong skeleton to hold them up. (C)

MAKING ART (Performance)

a. Build the skeleton of an object with just one type of stick. (F)

b. Join all the pieces together firmly. (E)

c. Cover the skeleton shape you made. (E)

APPRECIATING ART (Affective)

Decide what parts of your skeleton to change to make it look better. (D)

Art Materials

Toothpicks, popsicle sticks, soda straws, or other simple stick shapes

Glue and applicator

Cellophane or plastic wrap

Scissors

Newspaper

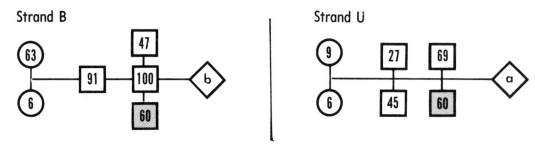

Strand B

63 — 91 — 100 — b
6   47
       100
       60

Strand U

9 — 27 — 69 — a
6   45   60

Lesson 60 — ROBBY THE ROBOT

A robot is a machine designed to do special jobs in the place of people. However, science fiction books and television have changed our ideas about robots. They have buttons and dials and flashing lights, but we see them mostly as machines with human features. They might even be considered pieces of moving sculpture.

Instructions

1. Collect some boxes and containers that you think would help you make your robot sculpture. Put your pieces together to make the weirdest, scariest, or funniest robot you can.

2. Add dials, lights, antennas, and levers to make the robot more interesting. Finish the robot by painting it. Lastly, stick on any extra pieces and draw in small details.

Escobar Marisol, "Women and Dog", 1964

72'' x 82'' x 16'', wood, plaster, synthetic polymer paint and miscellaneous items

Collection of Whitney Museum of American Art, New York, Gift of the Friends of the Whitney Museum of American Art

Lesson Objectives
MAKING ART (Performance)
   a. Build a robot out of boxes and other containers. (F)
   b. Add details to finish the robot sculpture. (F)

Art Materials
A collection of cartons, boxes, and other containers
Masking or cellophane tape
Paints
Colored cellophane, aluminum foil, colored paper
Glue and applicator
Crayons or felt tip markers
Newspapers

Strand E

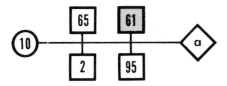

Lesson 61 — CHINA AND JAPAN

Poetry and painting were important in China, because people knew that artists and poets did a lot of very careful thinking. And the Chinese believed this was a good thing to do. But Chinese artists did not go outside and draw what they saw. They first learned how to draw by studying exactly how great artists before them had drawn and painted. The best art was made to look like other art, not always the way things really looked.

Japanese artists became very good at making brightly-colored pictures by printing with blocks of wood that had been specially cut. Japanese prints are noted for their simple lines and coloring.

Chinese and Japanese artists also designed beautiful buildings, carved sculpture, made jewelry, embroidered beautiful clothes, and built great gardens. But this lesson is just about picture making.

Instructions

1. Look at the Chinese and Japanese artworks that go with this lesson. Also look at the color pictures by the Chinese artist Shen Chou (20B) and the Japanese artist Hokusai (18B). Chinese painting has carefully-made lines and dabs made with a soft brush. The colors are usually soft and grayish. Japanese prints are made with large colorful spaces, sometimes with black outlines.

2. See how well you can copy one of the artworks. Try to learn how to make your work exactly like the artist's. Look and see the ways the Chinese artist made marks with the brush. Or see how the Japanese artist put the detail just where it was needed. You can use the ideas of other artists to improve your own art.

Hokusai, "Famous Bridges of the Provinces"

Wang Wen,

"Immortals and a Three-Legged Frog"

Lesson Objectives

UNDERSTANDING ART (Conceptual)

a. Learn that Chinese students studied art by copying the way great artists worked. (C)

b. Learn that Chinese and Japanese artists made beautiful buildings, sculpture, jewelry, embroidery, and gardens. (C)

MAKING ART (Performance)

Copy an artwork done in China or Japan. (F)

APPRECIATING ART (Affective)

Decide how much a copy is like the real artwork. (A)

Art Materials
Drawing paper
Paints
Brushes
Mixing tray
Water, paper towels
Pencil and eraser

Strand G

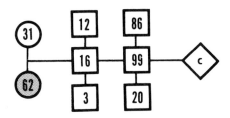

Strand M

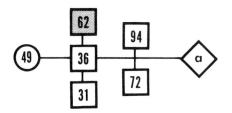

Lesson 62 — LEONARDO DA VINCI

Leonardo da Vinci lived over four hundred years ago in Italy. He was a genius*—he was an artist, a scientist, and an engineer. He had so many ideas that he filled up lots of notebooks with drawings and writing. He designed things like airplanes, bicycles, and machine guns that were not actually invented for hundreds of years. He also drew human bones and muscles to understand better how people were made. He designed buildings, painted pictures, made sculpture, and changed the way art teaching was done. He knew that writing down ideas was important. But he knew that drawing ideas was just as important.

Instructions

1. You can learn a lot about art by studying the work of great artists. Look at the photographs of da Vinci's drawings. Choose one that you like and think you can draw.

2. Copy the drawing on a piece of paper as carefully as you can. If you can't get the main shape right, you can trace (†) it first. But only trace the main outline. Fill in all the details yourself.

3. Look at the color picture by da Vinci (15A) to see how he painted.

*The meaning of this word is in the Glossary. (232-236) † For an explanation turn to the How To Do It section. (237-250)

Leonardo da Vinci, "Oak Leafs with Acorns and a Spray of Greenwood"

Reproduced by Gracious Permission of Her Majesty the Queen
Royal Library, Windsor

154

Leonardo da Vinci, "Five Grotesque Heads"

Reproduced by Gracious Permission of Her Majesty the Queen   Royal Library, Windsor

Lesson Objectives
UNDERSTANDING ART (Conceptual)
    a. Learn that Leonardo da Vinci was a genius. (C)
    b. Learn that da Vinci put his many ideas down in notebooks. (C)
MAKING ART (Performance)
    Copy one of da Vinci's drawings. (A)
APPRECIATING ART (Affective)
    Decide how much your drawing is like the one by Leonardo da Vinci. (A)

Art Materials
Pencil and eraser
Drawing paper
Tracing paper

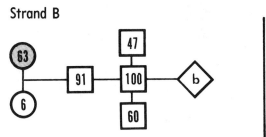
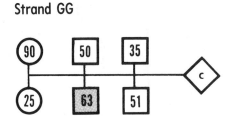
Lesson 63 — RELIEF MAP SCULPTURE

Maps show what places look like from high above. Different colors are sometimes used to show different heights of the land. Some maps, called relief* maps, are actually built up to show hills and valleys. The different levels on the map are called contours*.

In this lesson you are going to invent a piece of relief sculpture. You will make contour levels by sticking pieces of cardboard or styrofoam together. Try to create the most interesting ways you can think of for building a cardboard relief.

Instructions

1. The pictures with this lesson may give you ideas for your own sculpture. Notice how parts are built up with smaller and smaller pieces. Notice how hollows are made. Each level can be painted a slightly different color to make the contours look better.

2. Cut flat pieces of corrugated cardboard or sheet styrofoam into shapes you like. Use a knife or a pair of scissors(†). If you cut with a knife, be sure to put thick cardboard underneath where you cut. Be sure to keep your fingers away from the blade.

3. Practice arranging the pieces in interesting ways on a flat piece of cardboard the size of your finished relief. Paint the parts that will show. Then glue all the pieces in place.

4. If you want to show hollows or deep holes in your relief, first cut the main shape in the cardboard base. Each level you go down has to be cut out of cardboard the same size as the base. When everything is cut out, paint the parts that will show. Then glue all of the pieces in place.

*The meaning of this word is in the Glossary. (232-236)   † For an explanation turn to the How To Do It section. (237-250)

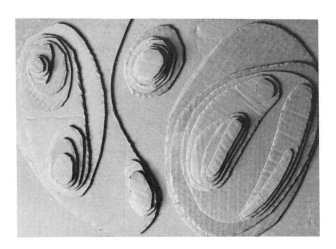

156

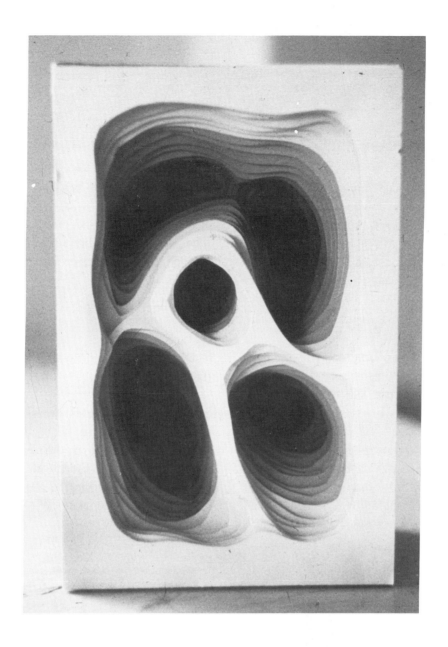

Lesson Objectives

UNDERSTANDING ART (Conceptual)

    a. Explain the meaning of contour as a change in the shape of something. (B)

    b. Explain the meaning of relief in art as sculpture that sticks out from a flat background. (B)

MAKING ART (Performance)

    Cut cardboard into shapes or cut holes in cardboard with scissors or a knife. (E)

Art Materials

Corrugated paper, corrugated cardboard, styrofoam sheets, such as from super-market food packaging

Scissors

Glue and applicator

Painting materials

Cutting knife

Heavy cardboard (to protect desk top)

Strand A

71 — 34 — 77 — ◇ a
84 — 39 — 44
64

Strand AA

64 — 82 — ◇ c
71 — 76 — 56

Lesson 64 — TWISTED SEEING

When you look through flat glass, everything looks all right. But if you look through a window or into a mirror that has curves and hollows in it, everything looks twisted out of shape. What you see is distorted*. Often the distortions are funny to look at.

In this lesson you are going to draw what you see. But your drawing will come out looking distorted. Artists use ideas like these in their work, even when they are not looking through curved glass or into curved mirrors.

Instructions

1. Find a fairly large photograph you like from a magazine. Carefully measure it into squares or rectangles that are all the same size. (See diagram 1.)

2. On a piece of white paper, draw an area the same shape and size as the whole picture. Divide this shape into the same number of spaces as on the photograph. But this time

The meaning of this word is in the Glossary. (232-236)

make all the spaces different sizes and shapes. (See diagram 2.)

3. Draw exactly what is in each of the squares on the photograph to fill in the new shapes you have made. Begin at the square with the X. Since the spaces are different, your drawing will look different from the photograph. It will be distorted, like looking in a curved mirror.

diagram 2

diagram 1

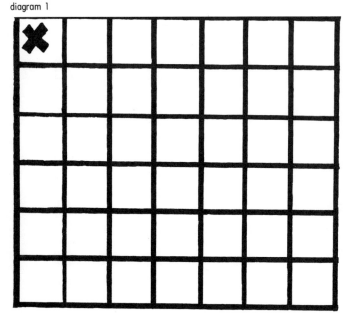

Lesson Objectives

UNDERSTANDING ART (Conceptual)
  a. Explain the meaning of distorted as a change in the way something looks to make it more interesting. (B)
  b. Learn that artists often use distortion in their work. (C)

MAKING ART (Performance)
  a. Divide a photograph into squares or rectangles. (F)
  b. Draw what you see in each square of the photograph to fill spaces of different sizes and shapes. (A)
  c. Make a drawing showing distorted shapes. (F)

Art Materials
Pencil and eraser
Ruler
White paper
Photograph from a magazine

159

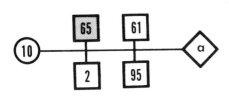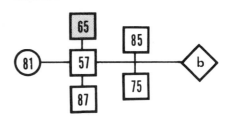
Lesson 65 — IN AND OUT OF FOCUS

If you look through glasses that belong to a person with bad eyesight, everything will look blurry. If you look through binoculars and the view is blurry, you can make everything look clear by twisting a knob. Then the view is in focus*. Our eyes focus on things that interest us so we can see them clearly. But the rest of what we see is not in focus.

Photographs often show just one part in focus. The rest is out of focus. Some parts are so blurry you cannot tell what they are.

In this lesson you are going to make a picture that has just one part in focus. All the other parts should be out of focus. Artists use focus to help people see the important parts of their pictures.

Instructions

1. Everyone has a place they would like to go to or things they would like to do when school is out. Make a picture that shows it. Draw the picture lightly with a pencil.

2. Decide which is the most important part of your picture. Then decide which parts are not very important at all. Draw the important parts in focus. They should be very sharp and clear. Draw the other parts out of focus. The parts of the picture that are less and

less important should be more and more blurry. Some parts should be so fuzzy that you cannot tell what is there. Use a crayon to color your work. Fill all the spaces in your picture.

3. The color pictures by Georges Seurat (21A) and J. M. W. Turner (25B) show some parts of their pictures in focus and other parts out of focus.

* The meaning of this word is in the Glossary. (232-236)

160

Lesson Objectives

UNDERSTANDING ART (Conceptual)

    a. Learn that the things we are looking at are clear and in focus and that everything else is blurry and out of focus.(C)

    b. Learn that artists use the idea of focus in their work to make it more interesting. (C)

MAKING ART (Performance)

    Draw a picture that shows the main part in focus and the other parts out of focus. (F)

APPRECIATING ART (Affective)

    Decide where to use the idea of focus to make your drawing look good. (D)

Art Materials
Drawing paper
Pencil and eraser
Crayons

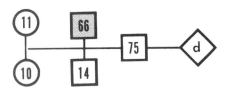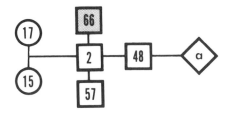
Lesson 66 — SPOOKY FOOD

How would you feel if you saw a hamburger that was green? Would you still want to eat it? Would you still be thirsty if your glass of milk turned blood red?

Artists are always surprising people with unusual looking things. They try to make us have new feelings. Sometimes what we see makes us laugh. At other times the artwork makes us feel horrible inside. But all these feelings are natural, and we need to learn about them.

Instructions

1. Draw the outline* shapes for a picture that shows a table with a meal on it. It could be at your home or at school. Try to remember all the kinds of food that are usually there. Draw the food so that it is the important part of your picture.

2. Paint the picture. But change some of the colors to make them very different. Think of a reason for changing the colors. Maybe you want to frighten people. Or you may want to make them feel sleepy.

3. Write down your reason for changing the colors. Put it on the back of your picture. If you had more than one idea, put all of them down.

* The meaning of this word is in the Glossary. (232-236)

Lesson Objectives

UNDERSTANDING ART (Conceptual)

    a. Learn that artists often change the colors of things to make us have new feelings about them. (C)

    b. Remember everything about a table with a meal set on it. (A)

MAKING ART (Performance)

    a. Draw everything you can remember about a table that has a meal set on it. (A)

    b. Paint a picture in colors that are not natural. (A)

APPRECIATING ART (Affective)

    Think of a reason for changing the colors of things in a picture. (C)

Art Materials
Paints
Brushes
Water, paper towels
Mixing trays
Paper
Pencil and eraser

163

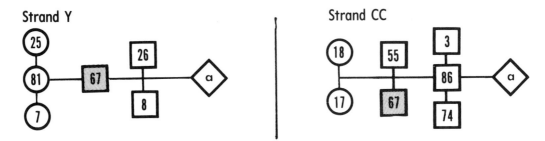

Strand Y

Strand CC

Lesson 67 — TRAIN YOUR VISUAL MEMORY

Everyone remembers some of the things he or she has seen. If you close your eyes, you can often see in your mind what something you know looks like.

You can improve your visual memory with practice. One of the best ways to do this is through drawing. This lesson is to help you train your visual memory.

Instructions

1. Find a picture you would like to draw. It should be about the size of a piece of drawing paper. You might want to use the pictures by El Greco (14B), Hiroshige (20A), Van Gogh (23), or Chagall (27B). Study the picture you choose very carefully.

2. Tear(†) a hole in a sheet of drawing paper so you take out about one-third of the paper. The paper should be the same size as the picture. The paper should be fairly thick so you cannot see through it.

3. Tape or clip the drawing paper over the picture. Draw from memory all the parts of the picture that are covered up. The part that isn't covered will help you. If you forget what part of the picture is like, take a look. Every time you have to look, make a mark on the back of your drawing.

4. Now draw the same picture again on another sheet of paper with very small holes in it. Test yourself again to see how much you can draw without looking.

† *For an explanation turn to the How To Do It section. (237-250)*

164

Lesson Objectives
UNDERSTANDING ART (Conceptual)
     Learn that people can improve their visual memory
     by drawing what they remember. (C)
MAKING ART (Performance)
  a. Tear holes in sheets of paper. (E)
  b. Draw parts of a picture from memory. (F)
APPRECIATING ART (Affective)
     Decide what picture you would like to draw. (D)

Art Materials
Drawing paper
Pencil and eraser

Strand C

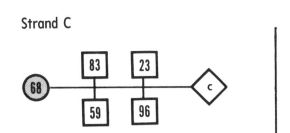

Strand T

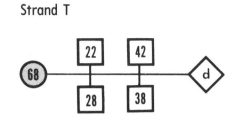

Lesson 68 — STRING ALONG WITH ART

String, silk thread, nylon fishing line, and thin wire make lines. If you just let them lie on a table top, they twist and turn in all directions. If you stretch them between two nails, they make a straight line. If you add more nails, you can make a design that is very interesting.

We don't often think of art being made with straight lines, but this is one way to do it that almost always makes good artwork.

Instructions

1. Hammer some brads* or linoleum tacks about halfway into a piece of plywood or wallboard. You can glue pieces of wood to the board to change the height. Hammer some tacks into these pieces as well. You may want to make all the tacks the same distance apart or spread them all over the board.

2. Tie one end of your string to one of the tacks. Stretch the string to another tack opposite it. Go around it clockwise and come back to another tack. Always keep your thread tight. As you go around more and more tacks,

* *The meaning of this word is in the Glossary. (232-236)*

you will see a design begin to grow. If you don't like what you have done, you can undo it.

3. Tie your thread when you have finished. You may want to use only one kind of line, or you may want to use two of three different kinds to make your design more interesting. Put some glue on the knots you tie to make sure they do not slip.

4. Look at the pictures that go with this lesson, but don't copy them.

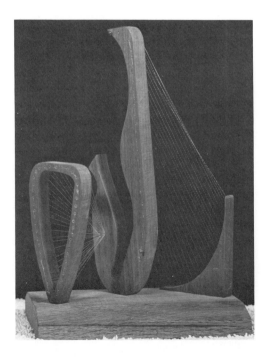

166

Barbara Hepworth, "Theme on Electronics (Orpheus)"

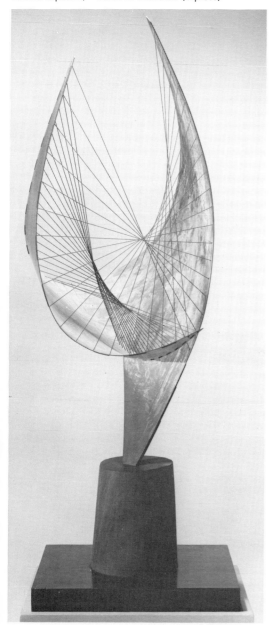

The Tate Gallery, London

Lesson Objectives
UNDERSTANDING ART (Conceptual)
    Learn that good art may be made just by using straight lines. (C)
MAKING ART (Performance)
  a. Hammer tacks into a board. (E)
  b. String thread around tacks to make a design. (F)
APPRECIATING ART (Affective)
    Choose the kinds of lines that make a design that you like. (D)

Art Materials
A piece of plywood or wall board
Glue and applicator
Brads or linoleum tacks
Thread, thin yarn, thin string, nylon fishing line, thin copper wire
Scissors
Wood scraps (optional)
Hammer

167

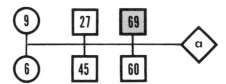

Lesson 69 — BRICKS AND BEEHIVES

A brick is a very simple object that has been used for thousands of years to build many different kinds of things. When you build with bricks, you are using the same shape over and over again to build many different kinds of shapes.

A beehive is made up of hundreds of small, hollow, waxy, box-like cells. Each cell in a beehive is the same shape.

A solid shape that is used over and over again, like a beehive cell or a brick, has a special name. It is called a module*. Many things in nature are made out of modules. Artists and designers often use modules in their work.

This lesson will give you the opportunity to build something artistic using modules.

Instructions

1. Decide on a simple object to use as a module in your work. Look at the Art Materials list for ideas.

2. Use your modules to build the craziest-looking piece of sculpture you can think of. All you have to remember is that the pieces must hold together firmly. If the sculpture is to stand up, then it must stand up easily. Most important of all, of course, is that it should look good.

3. Spray paint the finished sculpture if the modules have advertising print on them. Always use spray paint outdoors.

The meaning of this word is in the Glossary. (232-236)

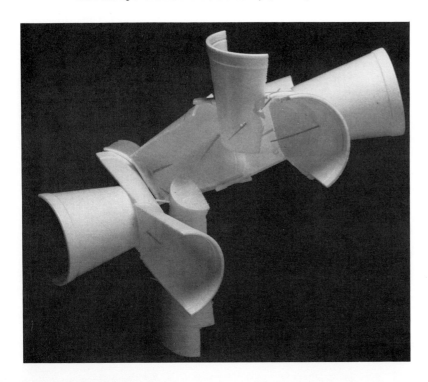

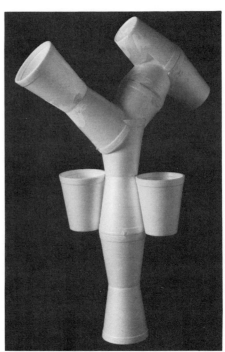

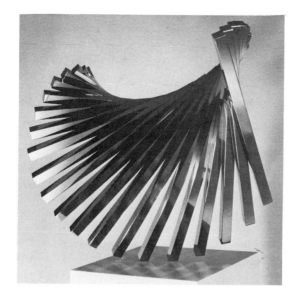

David Lee Brown, "1-76"

Indianapolis Museum of Art, Anonymous Owner

Raymond Rocklin, "Evocation"

Brass, 1958, Height: 66" Collection of the Whitney Museum of American Art, New York Gift of the Friends of the Whitney Museum of American Art

Lesson Objectives

UNDERSTANDING ART (Conceptual)
  a. Explain the meaning of a module in art as a simple solid object that is used over and over again to make a piece of sculpture. (B)
  b. Learn that modular construction is found everywhere in nature, and that people have used modules for thousands of years. (C)

MAKING ART (Performance)
  a. Build a piece of modular sculpture. (F)
  b. Attach objects together firmly. (E)

APPRECIATING ART (Affective)
  Decide that a piece of sculpture looks crazy, but good. (D)

Art Materials
A collection of solid objects to use as modules: foam cups, paper cups, egg cartons (cut or whole), cans, milk cartons, toilet paper roll centers (whole or sliced), pop bottles

A way to join modules together firmly: glue, wire, tape, staples

Can of spray paint

169

Strand S

76 20
    70 92 c
29 53

Strand BB

11 41 70
        92 d
25 13 95

Lesson 70 — JOHN MARIN'S NEW YORK

Whenever people think of New York City, they think of skyscrapers, the Statue of Liberty, museums, big ships, and Central Park. New York City is full of different kinds of art and design. One American artist painted the way New York looked and felt to him. His name was John Marin. He spent much of his life painting New York.

Other artists have also painted cities and towns. How would you paint or draw parts of your hometown to show the feelings that it gives you?

Instructions

1. Think about your hometown. What goes on there? Are there factories? Or railroads? Or big ships? Or truck stops? Is it a quiet place or a busy place? Is it smoky, cloudy, or sunny most of the time? Is it snowy or baking hot? How would you paint or draw the feelings you have about your town?

2. When you have finished your thinking, begin making quick pictures of your town. The first one may be just right. Or you may have to try a different view or different ways of painting to get just the right feeling. Finish the quick picture you like best. Make it just the way you want it to be.

John Marin, "The Red Sun, Brooklyn Bridge"

Courtesy of The Art Institute of Chicago

John Marin, "Woolworth Building"

Etching, 1913, Height: 13" x 10 3/8"
Collection of the Whitney Museum of American Art, New York

Lesson Objectives

UNDERSTANDING ART (Conceptual)

Learn that John Marin made many pictures about New York. (C)

MAKING ART (Performance)

a. Draw or paint quick pictures that tell about your hometown. (F)

b. Finish one picture about your hometown. (F)

APPRECIATING ART (Affective)

Decide which picture idea tells best how you feel about your town. (D)

Art Materials
Anything that you like to draw with
Anything that you like to paint with
Paper

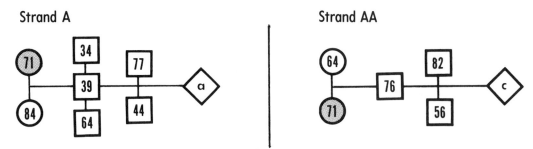

Strand A

Strand AA

Lesson 71 — MAKING DISTORTED IMAGES

People often say they are not good at art. This usually means they have not been given the proper help. There are lots of ways to make interesting art. This lesson tells you how to do one of them. You should end up laughing at the funny distortions* you make.

Instructions

1. Look in a magazine and find a large, clear photograph of a person or animal. With a pencil and ruler(†), mark the photograph into squares measuring 1½''.

2. Mark a piece of paper into oblongs. Make the same number of oblongs as there are squares on the photograph. The oblongs are to measure 1½'' across and 2½'' down.

3. Draw the shapes in the squares to fill each corresponding oblong on your paper. Notice how the picture stretches downward.

4. Mark out another piece of paper. This time, make the oblongs 2½'' across and 1½'' down. Draw the shapes of the photograph to fill the oblong shapes across. Shade in all parts.

*The meaning of this word is in the Glossary. (232-236)   † For an explanation turn to the How To Do It section. (237-250)

172

Lesson Objectives
UNDERSTANDING ART (Conceptual)
    a. Learn that you don't have to be gifted to make interesting art. (C)
    b. Explain the meaning of distortion as changing the way something looks to make it more interesting. (B)

MAKING ART (Performance)
    a. Draw 1½'' squares on top of a photograph. (E)
    b. Draw two sheets of 1½'' x 2½'' oblongs. (E)
    c. Transfer the outline shapes of a photograph to pieces of drawing paper. (E)
    d. Shade in the parts of a drawing to look more like the photograph. (A)

APPRECIATING ART (Affective)
    Decide which distortion best fits the photograph you chose. (D)

Art Materials
Pencil and eraser
Large photograph from a magazine
Ruler
Drawing paper

173

Strand M

```
      [62]
           [94]
(49)─[36]──────◇ a
      [31]  [72]
```

Strand R

```
      [35] [72]
(49)──────────◇ b
      [47] [73]
```

Lesson 72 — ACTION SPORTS

Basketball, track, boxing, wrestling, hockey, tennis, and gymnastics are all action sports. The players need to use certain exact movements. They usually need to move fast. What do the players look like as they make these movements? How do their bodies bend and twist when they dive, turn, jump, or kick? Make a picture of what goes on in one of these sports.

Instructions

1. Choose the kind of art materials that you would like to use. Choose the kind of sport that you like best.

2. Using the art materials you have chosen, show the players in action. Show how they look and feel when making these movements.

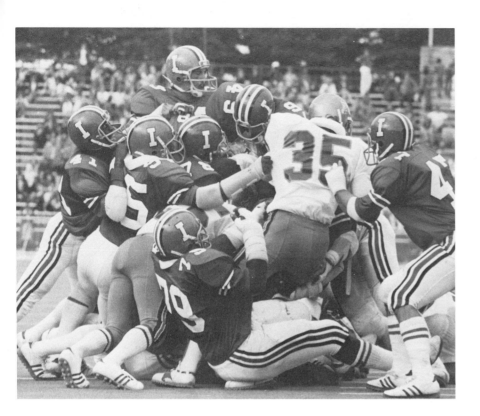

Finnish student

Lesson Objectives

MAKING ART (Performance)

    a. Make a piece of art that shows an athlete in action. (F)

    b. Make the parts of an athlete's body the proper shape and in the proper position. (A)

APPRECIATING ART (Affective)

    Choose the kind of art materials you would like to use for this lesson. (D)

Art Materials

Choose your own art materials

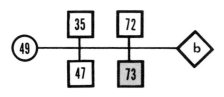
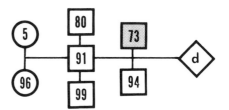
Lesson 73 — PEOPLE AT WORK

On some jobs people sit down. These jobs are not as interesting to observe as those jobs where people move about. What kinds of jobs do you know of that are interesting to watch? Construction workers climb scaffolding and dig deep holes. Dock workers load and unload trucks at depots. Can you think of other places where people are busy doing things? How do their bodies twist and bend as they work? In this lesson you will draw people working.

Instructions

1. Think of the kinds of work you would like to make into a picture. When you have decided on the kind of work you like, start working on your picture.

* The meaning of this word is in the Glossary. (232-236)

2. Make the part of the body required to do the work the center of interest*. The pictures that go with this lesson may help you, but use your own ideas as well.

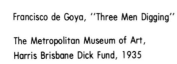
Francisco de Goya, "Three Men Digging"

The Metropolitan Museum of Art,
Harris Brisbane Dick Fund, 1935

176

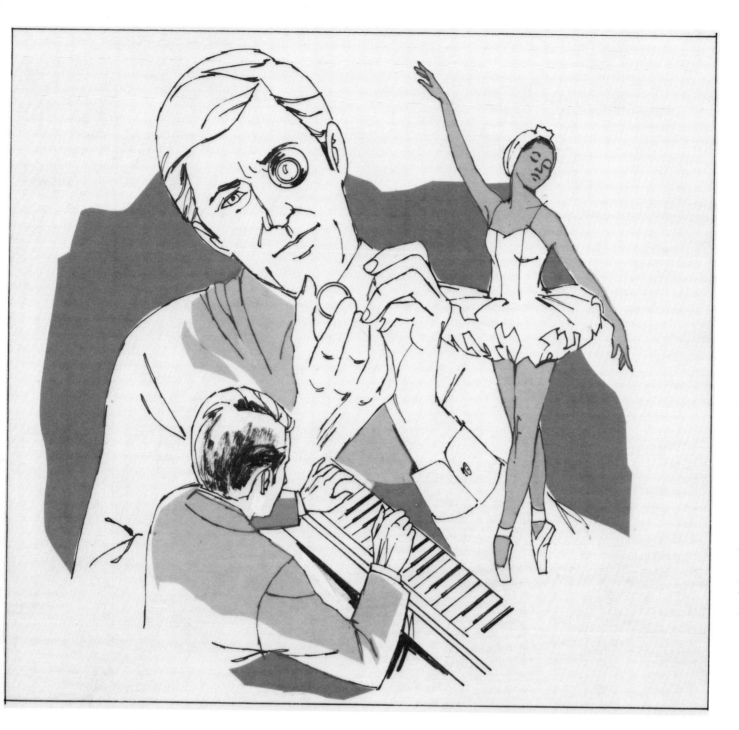

Lesson Objectives

UNDERSTANDING ART (Conceptual)

a. Explain the meaning of center of interest as the most important part of a work of art. (B)

b. Learn that people at work can be the subject of good painting. (C)

MAKING ART (Performance)

a. Make a painting of people doing a special kind of work. (F)

b. Show that you remember how people look by drawing and painting them. (A)

Art Materials
Drawing paper
Paint or crayons
Brushes
Mixing tray
Pencil and eraser
Water, paper towels

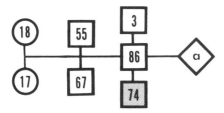

Lesson 74 — WHEN THE SPANISH CAME TO MEXICO

When Hernando Cortes landed on the shores of Mexico in 1519, the Indian people thought he was a white god. Even though he had only a very small army, he captured the great Aztec empire and Mexico became a colony of Spain. While the Spanish were rulers of Mexico, the art was a mixture of Indian and Spanish ideas. This kind of art lasted for over three hundred years. During this time large, decorated palaces and churches were built. Artisans made beautiful furniture, jewelry, pottery, clothing, and pictures. In this lesson you will learn about this kind of art.

Instructions

1. Look at the pictures that go with this lesson. Choose one you like.

2. When you have chosen the one you like best, draw a picture of it. Drawing makes you look at things more carefully. Do the lines first. Try and put in every detail that is in the picture. When you have drawn all the lines, put in the shading.

Lesson Objectives

UNDERSTANDING ART (Conceptual)

 a. Learn that Hernando Cortes captured the Aztec empire. (C)

 b. Learn that Mexican colonial art is a mixture of Spanish and Indian art. (C)

MAKING ART (Performance)

 Make a drawing of some Mexican colonial art. (A)

Art Materials
Drawing paper
Pencil and eraser

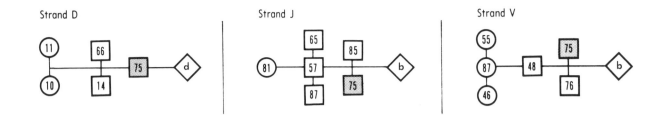

Strand D

Strand J

Strand V

Lesson 75 — CREATING ART FROM NIGHTMARES

Art tells about every kind of feeling we can have. One of these feelings is being scared. Bad dreams are called nightmares and can be very frightening. Some artists make all their work look like nightmares, because this is the best way for them to be creative. Here is your chance to try creating art from a nightmare you might have had.

Instructions

1. Think of something very scary. Think about how it would look if you put it into a picture.

2. When you have thought about your nightmare, draw and paint a picture about it. Use any color of paper you like for your picture.

3. If you want, you can add pieces of photographs. You can stick on scraps of colored paper, cloth, wood, aluminum foil, or anything you like that would make it scary.

4. The color pictures by Albrecht Dürer (18A), Joan Miró (27A), and Richard Lindner (28A) show scary or weird things that you might see in a nightmare. The pictures that go with this lesson may give you some ideas for doing your artwork.

Sir Jacob Epstein, "Rock Drill"

The Tate Gallery, London

Salvador Dali, "Apotheosis"

Indianapolis Museum of Art. Gift of Mr. and Mrs. Lorenzo Alvary

Martin Schongauer, "Saint Anthony tormented by Demons"

The Metropolitan Museum of Art, Rogers Fund, 1920

Lesson Objectives
UNDERSTANDING ART (Conceptual)
a. Learn that some artists make artwork that is scary. (C)
b. Learn that only the artist can know how things look in his or her dreams. (C)

MAKING ART (Performance)
  Draw and paint a picture that shows what a nightmare looks like to you. (F)

APPRECIATING ART (Affective)
  Choose your scariest nightmare idea for a picture. (D)

Art Materials
Construction paper (various colors)
Pencil and eraser
Glue and applicator
Scissors
Scrap materials
Paints
Brushes
Mixing trays
Water, paper towels

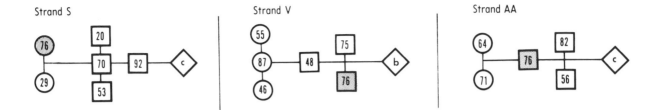

Strand S

Strand V

Strand AA

Lesson 76 — NEGATIVE IMAGES

Look at the photographs that go with this lesson. One of them looks quite unusual. All the dark parts are light and all the light parts are dark. Photographs like this are called negatives*. Normal photographs are called positives*. Have you ever thought what it would be like to make a picture all of negatives? Think about it! The shapes would stay the same, but the dark spots would become light. The bright colors would become dull. You will make a picture using negative images.

Instructions

1. Draw outlines for a painting of a scene you know well.

2. Paint the picture so that everything is opposite from the way it looks normally.

The meaning of this word is in the Glossary. (232-236)

3. Put in as much detail as you can. Look at the photographs that go with this lesson to get an idea of how your picture will look. They are black and white, so they will not tell you what to do with your colors.

Lesson Objectives

UNDERSTANDING ART (Conceptual)

a. Explain the meaning of positive in photography as a picture that shows the light and dark parts we see normally. (B)

b. Explain the meaning of negative in photography as a picture that shows all the light and dark parts the opposite from the way we normally see them. (B)

MAKING ART (Performance)

a. Paint a picture using negative images. (A)

b. Paint a picture showing every possible detail. (A)

Art Materials
Drawing paper
Paints
Brushes
Mixing tray
Pencil and eraser
Water, paper towels

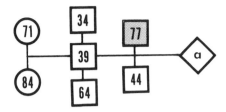
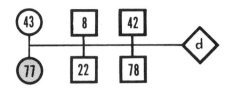
Lesson 77 — IMPOSSIBLES

People's eyes can play tricks on them so that impossible things seem to happen. Some artists like to use these kinds of ideas in their art. One of them was M. C. Escher, who lived in Holland. Escher created strange-looking scenes from his imagination that seem quite real until you look closely at them. If you think you would like to be creative using impossible looking arrangements, do this lesson.

Instructions

1. Choose one of the impossible arrangements that go with this lesson and use it to help you draw a picture of something that could never really happen that way.

2. Finish the picture by painting or coloring it. The pictures that go with this lesson may give you some ideas, but you must use your own ideas as well.

M. C. Escher, "Relativity"

184

The National Gallery of Art, Washington, D. C., Rosenwald Collection

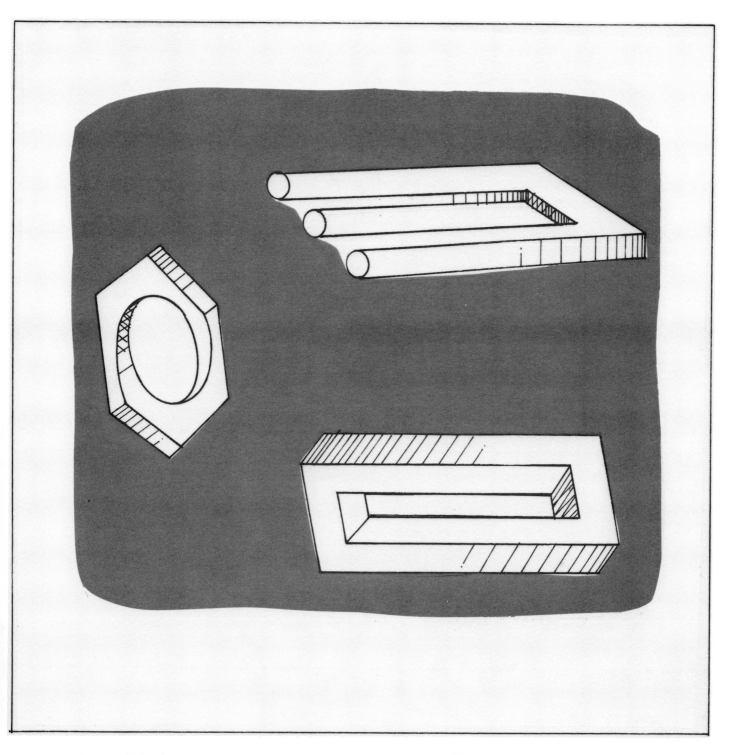

Lesson Objectives

UNDERSTANDING ART (Conceptual)

Learn that some artists like to have their work show things that are really impossible. (C)

MAKING ART (Performance)

a. Use an impossible arrangement to make a picture of a scene that may never happen. (F)

b. Finish your picture by painting or coloring it to make it look better. (F)

Art Materials
Pencil and eraser
Drawing paper
Paints, crayons, felt tip markers

185

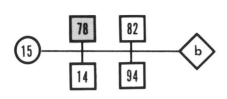
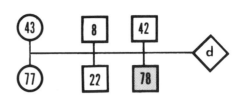
Lesson 78 — CREATIVE STARS AND STRIPES

The U. S. flag is made up of stars and stripes arranged in a special way. Have you ever thought of other ways of making designs with stars and stripes? In this lesson you will think of a creative* way to make a design using stars and stripes, along with the colors red, white, and blue.

Instructions

1. Practice drawing a five-pointed star like the one below. First draw a straight line, see (a) below. Draw line (b) down from line (a). Draw line (c) up through line (a). Take line (d) back down through lines (a) and (b). Join line (d) to line (a). Now you have a star.

2. Draw little ideas for designs using just stars and stripes. Put down as many ideas as

you can think of. You should have at least ten ideas for designs.

3. Choose the most creative design. Draw it to fill a large piece of paper. Then color it with red, white, and blue paint or crayon. The pictures that go with this lesson may give you some ideas.

* The meaning of this word is in the Glossary. (232-236)

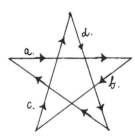

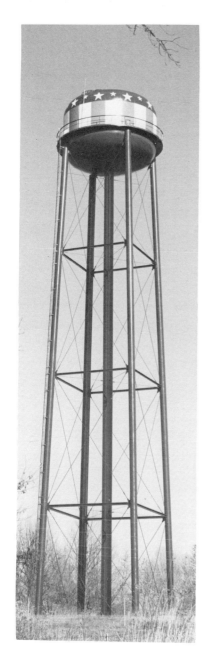

Alice Nichols, "Flagscape in Mesa Country"

Lesson Objectives

UNDERSTANDING ART (Conceptual)
- a. Learn that creative people have many ideas. (C)
- b. Explain the meaning of creative as making something with imagination. (B)

MAKING ART (Performance)
- a. Make many quick drawings of different stars and stripes designs. (A)
- b. Fill a piece of paper with a large, finished stars and stripes design. (F)
- c. Paint a design with red, white, and blue. (F)

APPRECIATING ART (Affective)

Choose the most creative stars and stripes design you made. (D)

Art Materials
Pencil and eraser
Paper
Crayons
Paints
Brushes
Mixing tray
Water, paper towels

187

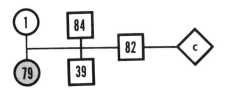

Strand O

Strand FF

Lesson 79 — WHAT IS A 3/4 VIEW?

When you look straight into a mirror, you see a front view of your own face. A ¾ view of a face is when you see someone from halfway between the front and the side. This kind of view shows part of the front and side together. It tells more about how someone looks than just a side view or a full-face view. Drawing ¾ views of people takes practice. The English artist Hans Holbein was very good at drawing ¾ view portraits*. Holbein lived four hundred years ago in the time of Henry VIII. You can learn a lot about how to draw faces from looking closely at portraits like these. It is your turn to draw a ¾ view portrait.

Instructions

1. Find a friend who will sit still and be drawn. Find the exact front view of your friend's face. Next find the side view. Move your friend to a position halfway between the two. This should be a ¾ front view.

2. Draw in the main shape of the head. Ask yourself these questions: Is the head as wide as it is high? Is it narrower than it is high? Are the eyes about halfway down the head? Are the ears at the same level as the eyes? How long is the nose? How wide is the mouth?

The meaning of this word is in the Glossary. (232-236)

3. When all the parts of the face are in their right places, put in the shading. When you do the shading, try to make the head look nice and solid. The pictures that go with this lesson may help your work.

4. The color pictures by El Greco (14B), Roger van der Weyden (17A), Hans Holbein (16), and Rembrandt (17B) show artists that have made ¾ view portraits. They may give you more help with your portrait.

188

Gilbert Stuart, "George Washington"

The Metropolitan Museum of Art, Gift of H. O. Havemeyer, 1888

Lesson Objectives
UNDERSTANDING ART (Conceptual)
    a. Learn what a ¾ view portrait looks like. (C)
    b. Explain the meaning of portrait as a work of art
       that shows a person's face. (B)
MAKING ART (Performance)
    a. Draw a ¾ view of a friend. (F)
    b. Make all the parts of a face in their proper posi-
       tion. (A)
    c. Make the shading show the head looking solid. (A)

Art Materials
Pencil and eraser
Drawing paper

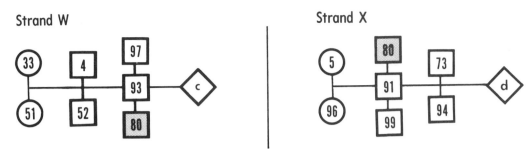

Strand W

Strand X

Lesson 80 — HENRY MOORE THE SCULPTOR

One of the most famous English sculptors is Henry Moore. He carves figures of people, but they do not look very real. He likes to change the usual shapes of the human body into something quite different. Sometimes parts of bodies are all joined together. His sculpture is always smooth and rounded. It makes you want to touch and feel the rounded shapes he made. All the parts seem to belong together. Try this lesson if you want to make some smooth, rounded sculpture yourself.

Instructions

1. Mix some plaster(†) in an empty milk carton. You can use clay(†) for carving.

2. Look at the pictures of sculpture by Henry Moore to give you some ideas.

3. Carve your plaster or clay into the shape of an animal or person lying down. Do your sculpture as Henry Moore would. To begin with, cut very little plaster away. Cut more away when you are sure how your finished sculpture will look.

4. When you have almost finished, make sure all the parts are round and smooth. Be sure all the parts seems to belong together, and that it still looks a bit like a person or an animal.

† For an explanation turn to the How To Do It section. (237-250)

Henry Moore, "String Figure"

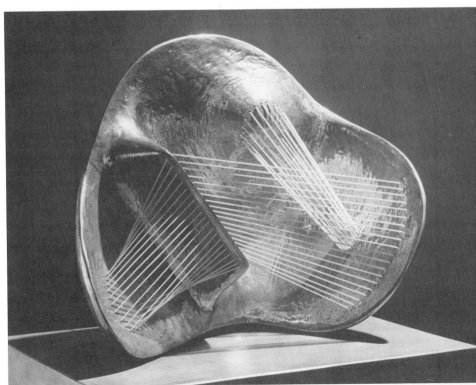

190

Henry Moore, "Reclining Figure"

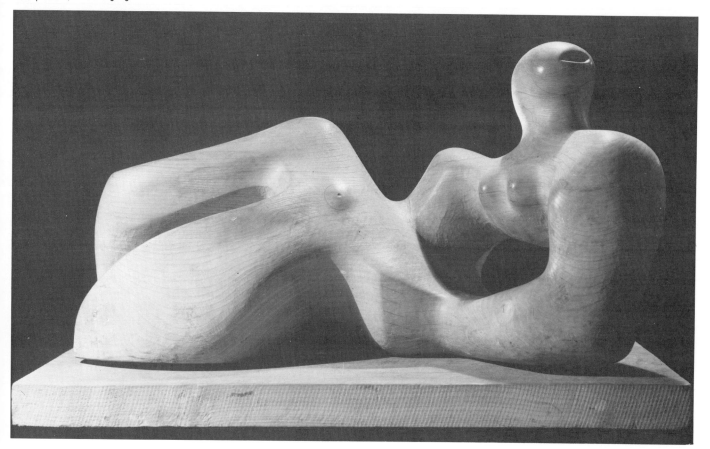

Albright-Knox Art Gallery. Buffalo, New York
Room of Contemporary Art Fund, 1939

Lesson Objectives
UNDERSTANDING ART (Conceptual)
   a. Learn that Henry Moore is a famous English sculptor. (C)
   b. Learn that Henry Moore changes the usual shape of people into something quite different. (C)

MAKING ART (Performance)
   a. Mix plaster. (E)
   b. Carve a block of plaster like Henry Moore would. (A)
   c. Make a piece of sculpture of a person or animal lying down. (F)

APPRECIATING ART (Affective)
   a. Decide whether your sculpture is made like Henry Moore does his. (A)
   b. Decide if all the parts are smooth and round. (A)
   c. Decide if all the parts seem to belong together. (D)

Art Materials
Plaster of paris
Bowl
Kitchen knife
Sandpaper
Clay
Water, paper towels
Newspaper

191

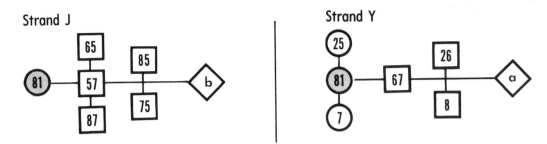

Strand J

Strand Y

Lesson 81 — DIFFERENT WAYS OF DRAWING

Every artist draws differently. Some draw every detail very carefully, others scribble their ideas down quickly. Some artists like to use thick, heavy lines, others like thin, wispy lines best. Most good artists can draw in several different ways, because a happy picture needs a different kind of drawing than a sad picture. They also know which ways they draw best when they use crayon, brush, or pen and ink, as well as different kinds of pencils. A good way to learn about different ways of drawing is to imitate how famous artists draw. Then you can mix different ways together to invent your own style*. Style means the way of making art that is especially yours.

Instructions

1. Find an interesting object that you would like to draw. It could be in your classroom or at home.

2. Look at the drawings that go with this lesson. Look through the book for other ways of drawing. Draw your object in the same style the artist used in his or her drawing.
* The meaning of this word is in the Glossary. (232-236)

3. Draw the same object twice more. Each time try using the drawing style of a different artist. Keep doing your drawing until you get it looking right. The color pictures by Nancy Singleton (13A), Hans Holbein (16), Albrecht Dürer (18A), Shen Chou (20B), and Henri Matisse (25A) all show very different styles of drawing.

Rembrandt, "A Cottage among Trees"

The Metropolitan Museum of Art,
The H. O. Havemeyer Collection.
Bequest of Mrs. H. O. Havemeyer, 1929.

Jacques Villon, "Portrait of Felix Barre"

The Metropolitan Museum of Art,
Purchase, 1963, Rogers Fund.

Lyonel Feininger, "Mid-Manhattan"

The Metropolitan Museum of Art,
George A. Hearn Fund, 1953

Lesson Objectives
UNDERSTANDING ART (Conceptual)
   a. Learn that good artists work hard to discover the ways of drawing that are best for them. (C)
   b. Explain the meaning of style in art as the special way an artist does his or her work. (B)

MAKING ART (Performance)
   Practice drawing in the same styles as three different artists. (A)

APPRECIATING ART (Affective)
   Choose three drawing styles that you think are interesting to look at. (D)

Art Materials
Pencil and eraser
Pen and ink
Brush
Paints
Drawing paper
Crayons
Water, paper towels

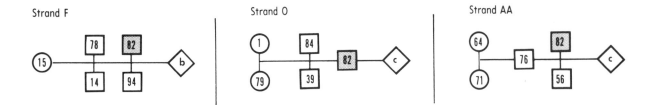

Strand F

Strand O

Strand AA

Lesson 82 — BE YOUR OWN PICASSO

Pablo Picasso was born in Spain but lived most of his life in France. He lived to be ninety-two and died in 1973. One of the special things about Picasso was the different styles* of art he used during his life. Many artists discover a way of doing their art that seems best to them, and then never change. Picasso did not do this. He kept on trying new ways of working. When you study his work, it is like looking at art by three or four different artists. In this lesson you will try being like Picasso.

Instructions

1. Think carefully about how you usually do your work in art. Make a piece of artwork that is done differently from the way you usually work. It should look as though it were done by someone else.

2. Be sure that what you do is more than just a change in the art materials you use.
* *The meaning of this word is in the Glossary. (232-236)*

You must try hard to change the way you paint or the way you do sculpture.

3. The pictures that go with this lesson show some of the different ways in which Picasso worked. This may help you make your own art different from what you normally do.

Pablo Picasso, ''The Cock''

The Tate Gallery, London

The Chicago Picasso

Pablo Picasso, "Head of a Woman"

Courtesy of The Art Institute of Chicago

Pablo Picasso, "The Tragedy"

The National Gallery of Art, Washington, D. C.
Chester Dale Collection, 1962

Pablo Picasso, "Mandolin and Guitar"

The Solomon R. Guggenheim Museum, New York.

Lesson Objectives

UNDERSTANDING ART (Conceptual)

    a. Learn that Pablo Picasso worked in many different art styles during his life. (C)

    b. Learn that Picasso was always trying new ideas in his art. (C)

MAKING ART (Performance)

        Make a piece of art that is done in a different style from the one you usually use. (A)

Art Materials
Choose your own art materials

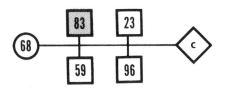
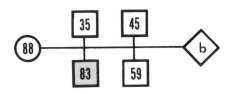
Lesson 83 — SCULPTURE MADE WITH LINES

Sculpture is art that is solid. Drawings are made with lines that are flat. See how you can make sculpture out of lines. The sculpture that is shown with this lesson is made with wire. Wire is a kind of line. It is long and thin, and wire is stiff. It can stand up by itself if it is bent. Sculpture like this is really solid sculpture made with wire lines. The wire can be wound around tightly or it can be open-spaced and loose. All artists have their own ways of doing things, and everyone thinks differently about how to make wire sculpture. How would you make yours?

Instructions

1. Wind some fairly stiff wire several times around a drinking glass, preserve jar, or a pop bottle. Gently take the wire off the object without spoiling the shape it has made.

2. Now make your own piece of solid-looking wire sculpture. When it is almost finished, hang it from a piece of thread. Be sure it looks right from every position.

Reg Butler, "Study for Woman Resting"

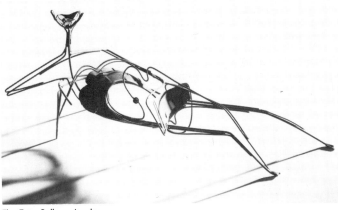

The Tate Gallery, London

H. Kramer, "Torso"

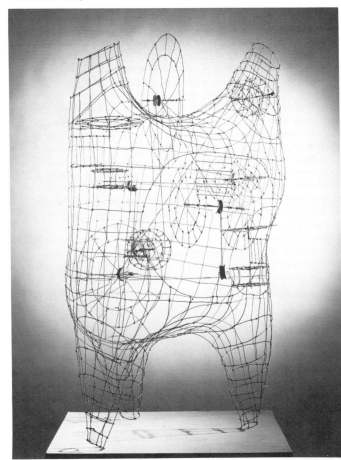

The Tate Gallery, London

196

Alexander Calder, ''Marion Greenwood'' (1929-30)

Brass wire, 12 5/8 x 11 1/8 x 11 3/8''.
Collection, The Museum of Modern Art, New York. Gift of the artist.

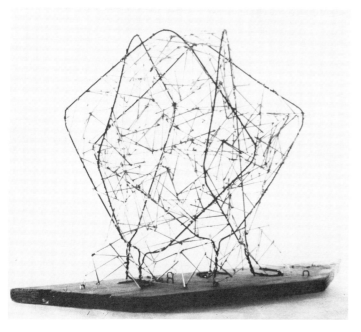

Lesson Objectives
UNDERSTANDING ART (Conceptual)
    Learn that bent wire can be made into solid sculpture. (C)
MAKING ART (Performance)
    Make a piece of wire sculpture. (F)
APPRECIATING ART (Affective)
    Decide when your sculpture looks good from all positions. (D)

Art Materials
Stiff wire
Thread
Thumbtack
Pliers for bending wire

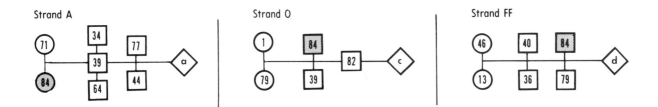

Strand A
Strand O
Strand FF

Lesson 84 — ART FROM INVENTED FACES

Maybe you have held your hand up in front of a fire or a lamp and watched the shadow. You can show the heads of animals in this way. Two hands together make even more interesting head shapes. You can make animal heads and human heads. Learning how to make these head shapes does not take very long. The illustrations* that go with this lesson show you some ways to make shadow heads.

Instructions

1. Practice making shadow heads. What kind of interesting picture could your shadow heads belong in? Could you invent* bodies to draw onto the heads? Could you draw in the rest of the picture to fit the animals you have drawn?

* *The meaning of this word is in the Glossary. (232-236)*

2. Make your drawing. When the drawing is completed, shade it in or color it with paint or crayon. This lesson helps you be creative*. You have to build a picture from the beginning, using your own ideas.

Lesson Objectives

UNDERSTANDING ART (Conceptual)

Learn that creative people put their own ideas together in unusual ways. (C)

MAKING ART (Performance)

a. Make shadow heads by holding your hands in different ways. (E)

b. Arrange heads with bodies and other things to make an unusual picture. (A)

Art Materials
Drawing paper
Pencil and eraser
Crayons, oil pastels, or painting materials

199

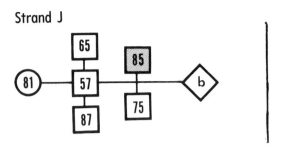
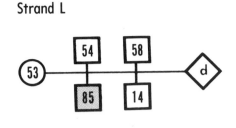
Lesson 85 — WEIRD VIEWS OF THINGS

Have you ever seen a strange view of something and didn't know what it was? Even a pencil looks different, if you hold it so the sharp point is exactly facing you. You might not recognize a picture of the underside of your kitchen table at home. Some things look better from unusual positions. A cloverleaf road junction on a freeway will often look much nicer from a helicopter than when you see it through a car window. Artists are always looking for unusual ways of showing things. In this lesson you have to draw an unusual view of something you know.

Instructions

1. The best way to do this lesson is to put yourself in the place where you can see an unusual view. Then draw what you see. You can climb under a sink or lie on your back and look at the ceiling. There are many unusual ways of looking at things.

2. When your drawing is as good as you can make it, shade it in. Only the perfectly white parts will be the color of your paper. Everything else will be shaded in with different grays. Only the very darkest parts will be shaded black.

200

M. C. Escher, "Hand with Reflecting Sphere"

The National Gallery of Art, Washington, D. C.
Gift of C. V. S. Roosevelt

Lesson Objectives
UNDERSTANDING ART (Conceptual)
  Learn that artists look for unusual views of things to make their pictures more interesting. (C)

MAKING ART (Performance)
  a. Draw an unusual view. (F)
  b. Fill in your drawing with different shades of gray. (A)

APPRECIATING ART (Affective)
  Choose a view of something that you think is interesting or unusual. (D)

201

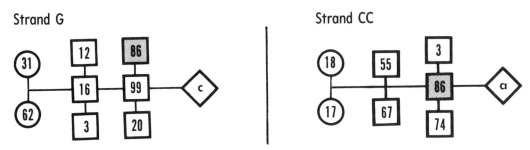

Strand G

Strand CC

Lesson 86 — ORIENTAL-AMERICAN ARTISTS

Chinese and Japanese people first came from their homelands to live in the Pacific coast states. They now live in many different states in the United States. Some have become famous artists and architects. This lesson is to help you get to know some of the work done by these artists.

Instructions

1. Look at the pictures of sculpture and painting by Oriental-American artists.

2. Make a clay model or a freehand* drawing of one of these artworks. Put in every detail you can see. Mark it number one.

3. Try to model or draw the same thing again from memory. Mark this number two. When you do this well, then you will really know the artwork you have chosen.

* The meaning of this word is in the Glossary. (232-236)

Isamu Noguchi, "Bird C (Mu)" (1952-58)

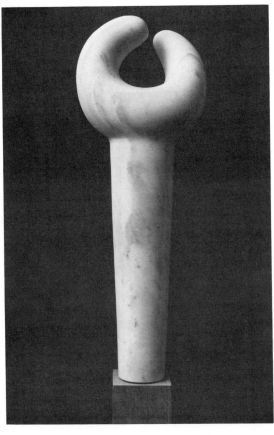

Greek marble, 22 3/4 x 8 1/8". Collection, The Museum of Modern Art, New York. Given anonymously, in memory of Robert Carson, architect.

Watercolor on paper. 21 x 29 3/8 inches. Collection of Whitney
Museum of American Art, New York.

Yasuo Kuniyoshi, "Juggler" (1952)

Ink on cardboard. 22 x 28 inches. Collection of Whitney Museum of Art,
New York. Purchase.

Lesson Objectives
UNDERSTANDING ART (Conceptual)
   a. Learn that the families of some famous American
      artists came from China and Japan. (C)
   b. Learn that if you can model or draw something from
      memory, it shows you really know what it is like. (C)
MAKING ART (Performance)
   a. Make a model or a drawing that looks like a work
      of art. (A)
   b. Make a model or drawing from memory to look like
      a work of art. (A)

Art Materials
Drawing paper
Pencil and eraser
Clay (oil or water base)

203

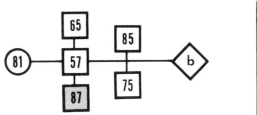
Lesson 87 — SHOWING REFLECTIONS

Reflections* show on calm water, mirrors, and any other smooth, shiny surfaces. Artists use reflections to make their pictures look good.

This lesson will help you learn to show reflections on water. Then you will know how to make your own pictures look more interesting.

Instructions

1. Imagine that you are looking across a river or a small lake. On the opposite shore is something that is interesting to look at. It could be a harbor or people fishing.

2. Draw your view on a sheet of paper. It should fill only the top half of your paper. Draw in only the outlines. The line showing where the water starts should be horizontal* and stretch from one side of your paper to the other.

3. Draw in the reflections of the things that are closest to the water. Make all the vertical*

* The meaning of this word is in the Glossary. (232-236)

lines in your picture stretch across the water toward you. These lines should stay vertical and stretch to the bottom of your paper. Draw in all the details in your reflections.

4. Paint your picture. The reflections will be painted the same color as the real things, but the reflections should fade much more toward the bottom of the picture. Even smooth water has little ripples on it. A way to show this is to paint or draw a few faint horizontal lines in white across your picture. The pictures that go with this lesson may give you some ideas.

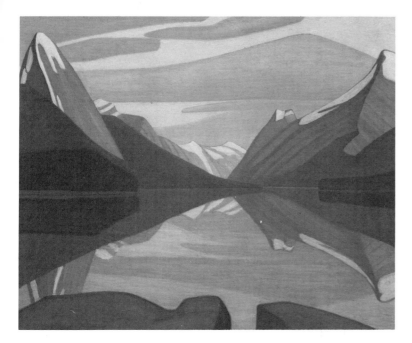

Lesson Objectives

MAKING ART (Performance)

    a. Draw a scene of something on the other side of a river or lake. (F)

    b. Draw in reflections on the water. (F)

    c. Paint in reflections with colors that are duller than the real things. (A)

APPRECIATING ART (Affective)

    Choose an interesting view. (D)

Art Materials
Drawing paper
Paints
Brushes
Mixing tray
Pencil and eraser
Water, paper towels

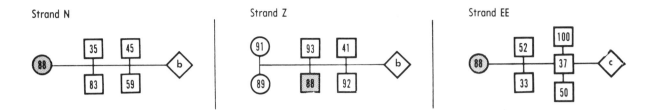

Strand N

Strand Z

Strand EE

Lesson 88 — REAL, NOT QUITE REAL, NOT REAL

People often wonder why some artists do work that looks unreal. The reason is that the shapes of real things often give artists ideas for new shapes. When the artist is finished, his or her shapes do not look real any more. The most important thing is that the artist is being creative. Being creative is more important than making things that look real.

Instructions

1. Look at the pictures that go with this lesson. They will help you understand how to change one shape into a new, more interesting shape. Find a photograph of an object, then draw or make a tracing(†) of it on paper.

2. Draw the same object on another sheet of paper. This time change the shape. It could be made simpler, or more complicated.

3. Do the same drawing again. Get your ideas from the second drawing you did. This final drawing should not look real at all. It should still be a bit like the real object you drew at first. Put your drawings together. Stick them onto a big piece of dark paper. Write on them "real," "not quite real," and "not real." Ask yourself if these words describe how your drawings look. The color pictures of paintings by Jan van Huysum (19), Vincent Van Gogh (23), and Jackson Pollock (26) show examples of real and not quite real artwork.

† *For an explanation turn to the How To Do It section. (237-250)*

Piet Mondrian, "Red Tree" (1908)

Collection, Haags Gemeentemuseum, The Hague, Holland

Piet Mondrian, "Tree" (1912)

Museum of Art, Carnegie Institute, Pittsburgh Maillil-Mondrian Fund

Piet Mondrian, "Composition in oval" (1914)

Collection, Haags Gemeentemuseum, The Hague, Holland

Piet Mondrian, "Composition with red, yellow and blue" (1921)

Collection, Haags Gemeentemuseum, The Hague, Holland

Lesson Objectives
UNDERSTANDING ART (Conceptual)
    Learn that artists often are being creative when they
    show things that look unreal. (C)
MAKING ART (Performance)
    Make three drawings of one object. Each drawing
    should look less real than the one before. (A)

Art Materials
Drawing paper
Tape
Dark construction paper
Pencil and eraser
Glue and applicator

207

Strand Q

Strand Z

Lesson 89 — ART DONE BY BLACK ARTISTS

All artists try to show the things they think are most important. Black artists in America sometimes make pictures about Black people. They show the places where Black people live and work. They show pictures of them in happy or sad moods. They show the great Black men and women. In this lesson you will make a picture like the Black artists have made.

Instructions

1. Look at the pictures by Black artists that go with this lesson. Notice the subjects they have chosen. Notice the ways in which they have shown their ideas.

2. Make a picture the way you think the Black artists would. It could be about the people, the neighborhood, the stores, the schools or anything else you might think of. When you have finished your picture, write a title* or a sentence to explain what your picture is about. You may wish to look at pictures by other Black artists for more ideas.

* *The meaning of this word is in the Glossary. (232-236)*

Charles White, "Preacher" (1952)

Ink on cardboard. 21 3/8 x 29 3/8 inches. Collection of Whitney Museum of American Art, New York

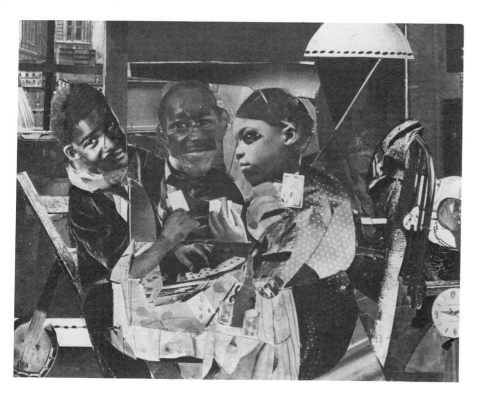

Romare Bearden, "Evening, 9:10, 461 Lenox Avenue"

Photo-enlarged panel, ca. 6 x 8', made from collages
included in exhibition "Projections,"
Cordier and Ekstrom, Inc., New York, October 6-24, 1964.
Photograph, Courtesy The Museum of Modern
Art, New York

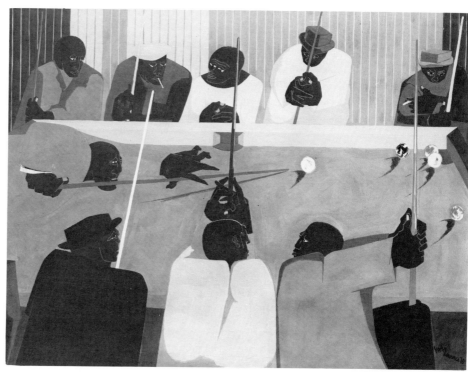

Jacob Lawrence, "The Pool Game" (1970)

Gouache. 21 5/8 x 29 1/2 inches.
Courtesy, Museum of Fine Arts,
Boston. Emily L. Ainsley Fund

Lesson Objectives
UNDERSTANDING ART (Conceptual)
   a. Learn that artists often paint about their own race
      or nationality. (C)
   b. Learn the names of three Black painters. (C)
MAKING ART (Performance)
   a. Paint a picture the way a Black artist would. (F)
   b. Explain your picture by giving it a title. (D)

Art Materials
Drawing paper
Paints
Mixing tray
Brushes
Pencil and eraser
Water, paper towels

209

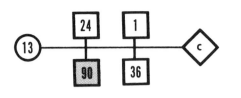
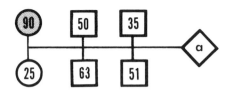
Lesson 90 — OUTSIDE SHAPES HAVE INSIDE SHAPES

If you were asked to draw a milk bottle or a baseball, you would start by drawing the outline of it. The outside is not its only shape. The space inside the outline also has some shapes. A good drawing sometimes will show the outside shapes as well as the inside shapes. One way to find out about the inside shapes of an object is to wind thick string or wool yarn around it. The lines of the string will show you the inside shapes; these inside shapes are called contours*.

Instructions

1. Wind some thick string around a simple, but interesting looking object. It could be a bat, a curvy vase, or a football. You should be able to see plenty of space between the lines made by the string or wool.

The meaning of this word is in the Glossary. (232-236)

2. Draw an outline of the object. Fill the object in so that the outline shows a contour of the object as well. Be sure that you draw the shapes made by the string exactly as you see them. Watch for every curve.

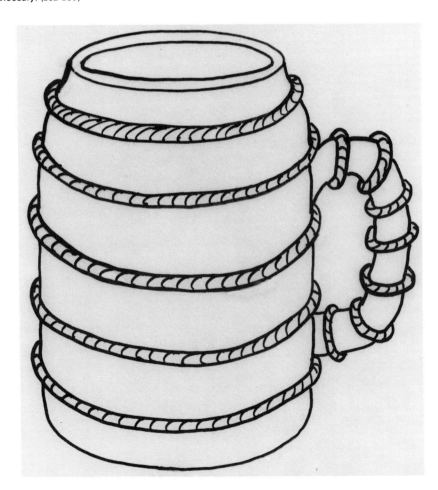

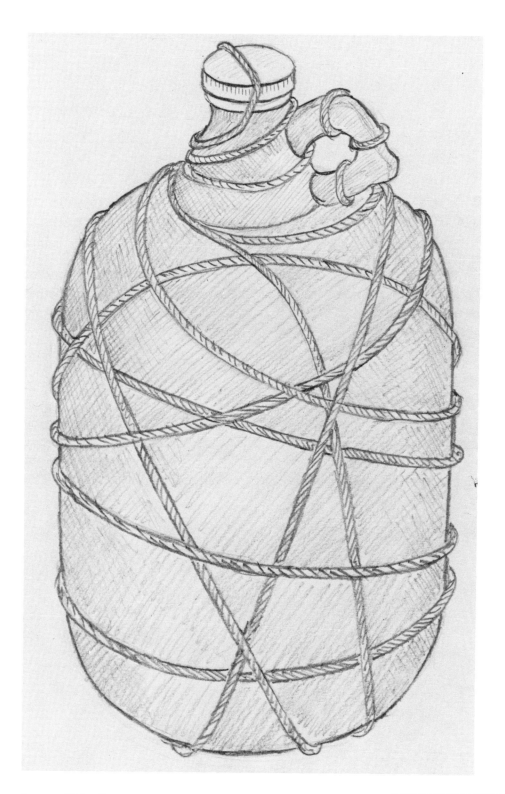

Lesson Objectives

UNDERSTANDING ART (Conceptual)

Explain the meaning of contour as the edge of any change of shape in an object. (B)

MAKING ART (Performance)

a. Make a contour drawing of an object. (F)
b. Choose an object to draw that shows different kinds of contours. (A)

Art Materials
Thick string or wool yarn
Pencil and eraser
Drawing paper
A simple-shaped object

211

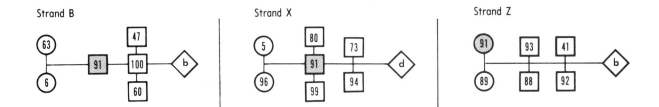

Strand B   Strand X   Strand Z

Lesson 91 — BLACK SCULPTORS

Black-American sculptors are making all kinds of sculpture. Black sculpture includes many forms and materials. Black-American sculptors create sculptures to communicate, to express their own ideas and feelings, or to make an object of beauty. One of the best ways to learn about what they do is to look at some sculpture by Black-Americans. Another very good thing is to use some of the same ideas they used in your own sculpture.

Instructions

1. Make a piece of sculpture. Get an idea for your own work from these Black sculptors. You could take an idea from one piece of sculpture and use it with an idea from another piece of sculpture. You might get an idea for your own art from just one sculpture.

2. Sculpture made of metal may give you ideas to do in paper or cardboard. Sculpture in stone might give you ideas for work in clay or plaster. If you wish, you might look at the work of other Black-American sculptors.

212

Richard Hunt, "Palmate Hybrid"

Indianapolis Museum of Art. Gift of the Alliance of the
Indianapolis Museum of Art

Arthur S. Rose, "Boy on a Dolphin"

Lesson Objectives
UNDERSTANDING ART (Conceptual)
    Learn that Black sculptors create sculptures in many
    different forms, using many different types of
    different forms and materials. (C)
MAKING ART (Performance)
    Make a piece of sculpture. (F)
APPRECIATING ART (Affective)
    Decide which art materials are best to use in your
    piece of sculpture. (D)

Art Materials
Choose your own art materials

213

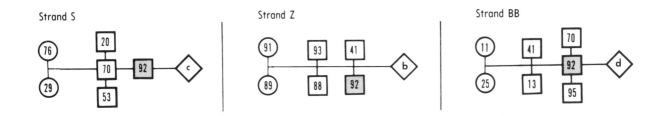

Strand S

Strand Z

Strand BB

Lesson 92 — ACTION

Most things around us move. Some things cause more excitement than others when they move. Stormy waves smashing against cliffs can be exciting. A horse race can be exciting.

Artists often do work that is exciting and full of action. In this lesson you will see how well you can show action in your art.

Instructions

1. Think about the kind of action you want to show. Decide on the kind of art that you think would be best for your idea. Choose any way of making art that seems right to you. It could be a drawing, a painting, or a collage.

2. Now do your action artwork. Make it as full of exciting action as you can. The color pictures by Titian (15B) and Hokusai (18B) show action.

Thomas Hart Benton, "Express Train" (1924)

Lithograph. 12 11/16 x 23 1/4 inches. Collection of Whitney Museum of American Art, New York.

Peter Paul Rubens, "The Lion Hunt"

Paolo Uccello, "Niccolo Mauruzi da Tolentino at the Battle of San Romano"

Lesson Objectives
UNDERSTANDING ART (Conceptual)
    Learn that artists often make art that is exciting
    and full of action. (C)
MAKING ART (Performance)
    Make some artwork that shows action. (F)
APPRECIATING ART (Affective)
    Choose the kind of art materials that will show your
    action idea best of all. (D)

Art Materials
Choose your own art materials

215

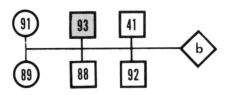
Lesson 93 — MODELING CLAY HEADS

When an artist paints a portrait, it is flat. A sculpture of a head is more like the real person, because it is solid. When a sculptor is making a model, he or she does more than show the shape of someone's head; the sculptor tries to show the kind of person he or she is modeling. This lesson helps you make a model of a head that shows human feelings.

Instructions

1. Make your clay(†) ready to use. If it is made with water, be sure it is well mixed. If the clay is made with oil, it will need to be made soft. This kind of clay gets soft if you bend and squeeze it in your hands.

2. Take half of your piece of clay and make it into an egg-shaped ball. Add a piece at the bottom for the neck. Stick clay on to make a nose, ears, and hair. Dig out parts to make the eyes. Look at the pictures that go with this lesson to make sure your head is the right shape from the front and sides.

3. Show the kind of person you are modeling. Is the person happy or sad, kind or cruel? It should be easy to see from the way you made the head.

† *For an explanation turn to the How To Do It section. (237-250)*

Jacob Epstein, "Albert Einstein"

The Tate Gallery, London

R. Brownell Mc Grew, "The Navajo, Tse Geddie"

Indianapolis Museum of Art. The Harrison Eiteljorg Collection
of Western American Art

Lesson Objectives
UNDERSTANDING ART (Conceptual)
   a. Learn that some clay is mixed with water and some
     is mixed with oil. (C)
   b. Learn that artists try to show what a person is like
     as well as how he or she looks. (C)
MAKING ART (Performance)
   a. Model a head in clay that shows all the parts in
     the proper places. (A)
   b. Show what kind of person you are modeling. (A)

Art Materials
Clay (water or oil base)
Newspaper
Plastic bags (to keep your
   work wet)

217

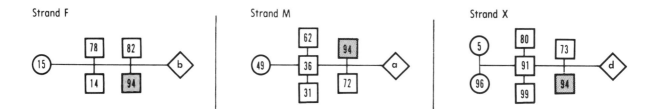

Strand F

78 82
15   b
14 94

Strand M

62
49 36 94 a
31 72

Strand X

80
5   73
96 91   d
99 94

Lesson 94 — GODS AND HEROES

Artists have always made pictures and statues of special people. The most important art is often about the different gods that people worship. Art is also made about the men and women who have done very brave things. These people are called heroes or heroines. Today we can find pictures of gods and heroes in comic books, on television, and in other places. This lesson is about making art that shows a god, goddess, hero, or heroine.

Instructions

1. Decide on a god, goddess, hero, or heroine that you would like to show in your art. It could show a hero or heroine from the comics or it could be an imaginary god. Your hero or heroine could be a soldier, a leader, or even a basketball player.

2. Decide on the kind of art you want to work in. You can draw, paint, model in clay, or work in any other way you like. Look at the gods and heroes shown in the color pictures by Pieter Breughel (14A), Leonardo da Vinci (15A), El Greco (14B), and Titian (15B).

Standing Ganesha

Courtesy of the Indiana University Art Museum

Chac, God of Rain

Hawk-headed Sphinx, Egypt

Lesson Objectives
UNDERSTANDING ART (Conceptual)
    Learn that artists have always shown gods, goddesses, heroes, and heroines in their work. (C)
MAKING ART (Performance)
    a. Make some art that shows a god, goddess, hero, or a heroine. (F)
    b. Invent a way of doing your art that you have not done before. (A)

Art Materials
Choose your own art materials

219

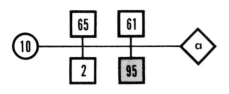

Strand E

Strand BB

Lesson 95 — PEACE

Art tells about the feelings that people have. Different artists have different ways of telling about the same kinds of feelings. One kind of feeling that everyone knows is peacefulness. An artist may be feeling quiet and peaceful and the picture will show his or her idea of peace. An artist may see a view of the way he or she feels and then paint it. People have many different kinds of feelings. Each person feels them differently. When people make pictures about how they feel, their work shows these different feelings.

Instructions

1. Sit still for a few minutes and think about the word peace. Think up pictures in your mind that fit the title.

2. Make a drawing or painting that tells about your feelings of peace. The color pictures by Rembrandt (17B), Hiroshige (20A), Georges Seurat (21A), Claude Monet (22A), Alfred Sisley (24B), and Paul Gauguin (24A) show peace in different ways. The pictures in this lesson also show a feeling of peace.

Hiroshige, ''Moonlit Night''

Roger van der Weyden, "Portrait of a Girl"

Lesson Objectives
UNDERSTANDING ART (Conceptual)
   Learn that people will have different feelings about the same subjects. (C)
MAKING ART (Performance)
   a. Make a picture about your idea of peace. (F)
   b. Make the picture fill the whole sheet of paper. (A)

Art Materials
White paper
Pen and ink
Crayons
Paints
Brushes
Mixing tray
Water, paper towels

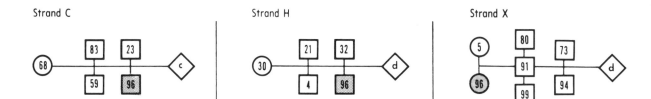

Strand C   Strand H   Strand X

Lesson 96 — BUILD THAT SCULPTURE BIG

Big sculptures are exciting to see. They are usually outdoors, in temples, or palaces. Artists usually make these big sculptures out of stone or metal. Sometimes big sculptures are painted. In this lesson your sculpture will be very big. It will be made of wood.

Instructions

1. Write down the name of a place where you think your large sculpture should go. Write down the kind of idea your sculpture should show. It could be a sculpture of a large animal for a zoo or a sculpture of an athlete for a stadium or anything else you wish to do.

2. Draw how you would like your idea for a sculpture to look. You can make it look real or you can make it look unreal.

3. Build your sculpture just as big as you can make it with solid wood and plywood. You can nail parts together; some can be held together with wire. Be sure it will stand up easily and the parts will hold together. Tin cans and other things can be nailed or wired on. The paint you use should be the kind used on the outside of a house. If the big sculpture is to go outdoors, you can use materials like chicken wire and cloth. If you add plaster of paris(†), the holes will fill in and become stiff. Stick a label onto your sculpture that tells what it is about. The pictures in this lesson show a big sculpture being built.

† *For an explanation turn to the How To Do It section. (237-250)*

Lesson Objectives

UNDERSTANDING ART (Conceptual)
 Learn that important sculpture is often very large. (C)

MAKING ART (Performance)
 Build a large piece of sculpture out of wood and other things. (F)

APPRECIATING ART (Affective)
 Decide on a place and a subject for your sculpture. (D)

Art Materials
Drawing paper
Pieces of wood
Wire
Paint
Brushes
Water (for water paints and latex)
Turpentine (for cleaning up oil paints)
Pencil and eraser
Hammer and nails
Pliers
Chicken wire, cloth, etc.
Plaster of paris
Tin cans, etc.

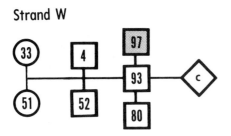

Lesson 97 — EMBOSSING

Silversmiths and goldsmiths often make relief* sculptures out of metal. Since gold and silver are very precious metals, they hammer the pictures out of thin sheets of flat metal. Some parts are hammered so they stick out, others are left almost flat. This lesson helps you emboss* your own relief using copper, brass, or aluminum foil. Foil is easier to shape than thicker metal sheets, and much cheaper than gold or silver.

Instructions

1. Draw a design of a person or place. Choose an idea that has some special feeling, such as war or peace. Make the design fill a shape the same size as your piece of metal foil.

2. When the design is done, lay the paper on top of the foil. Draw over the lines with a pencil. Press on it so the design shows through in the foil.

3. Make the person or place stick out by rubbing the back of the foil with a smooth stick. Add details such as eyes and hair. Also rub the relief from the top to stop it from wrinkling. Work on a pad of soft paper.

4. Another way of doing this lesson is to find objects that fit the shapes of your idea. Glue them onto cardboard. Spread the kind of aluminum foil used for cooking over the shapes. Gently rub the foil until the shapes underneath show through clearly. Spray or brush the finished art with clear or colored lacquer*. Different colored lacquers can make aluminum reliefs look good. Copper foil can be painted with a chemical called ammonium sulphide. Attach the embossed relief to a piece of wood or thick cardboard with pins or glue and hang it on the wall. The pictures that go with this lesson may give you some ideas.

*The meaning of this word is in the Glossary. (232-236)

Anthony Lauck, "Head of Christ"

Lesson Objectives
UNDERSTANDING ART (Conceptual)
    Explain the meaning of embossing in art as hammering
    or pressing a thin sheet of metal into a relief
    design. (B)
MAKING ART (Performance)
  a. Make an embossed relief out of metal foil. (F)
  b. Draw a design of a person or place to fill a sheet of
     foil. (A)
  c. Show shapes that have a special feeling, such as
     war or peace. (A)

Art Materials
Drawing paper
Pencil and eraser
Smooth modeling stick (pencil,
    spoon, etc.)
Water, paper towels
Piece of wood or thick
    cardboard
Glue for metal (epoxy)
Sheet of foil: aluminum, cop-
    per, brass
Pad of paper
Lacquer—clear and colored
Brush
Ammonium sulphide
Steel wool
Pins and hammer

225

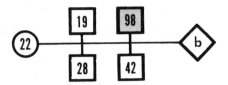

Lesson 98 — MACRAME

The word macrame* is French for knotted lace. It is an ancient way of weaving. Macrame designs are made by tying different knots in string to make a kind of textile* that has a lot of holes in it. Sailors on long sea voyages used to experiment with macrame knotting. Today many people make belts, handbags, vests, and wall decorations out of macrame. This lesson is just to get you started. There are many books on macrame. After you have done this lesson, you may want to go to the school library or to one in your community to get more ideas on macrame.

Instructions

1. Practice the five knots in this lesson until you can do each one without thinking about them. Practice tying them loosely and then tightly. Try them with hard and soft string.

2. Try repeating one of the knots until it makes a shape. One of the simplest things to make in macrame is a belt. If you want to, you can make an interesting design and hang it on the wall. Belts and wall hangings can also be made from a mixture of different kinds of knots. Look at the pictures in this lesson to get some ideas.

* The meaning of this word is in the Glossary. (232-236)

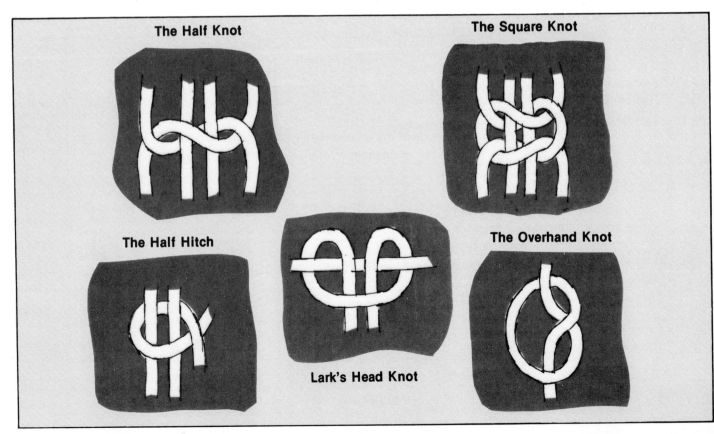

The Half Knot

The Square Knot

The Half Hitch

Lark's Head Knot

The Overhand Knot

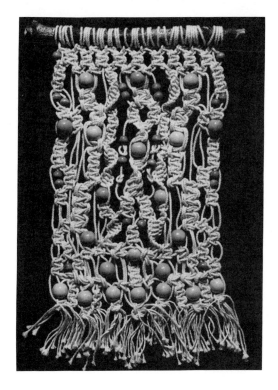

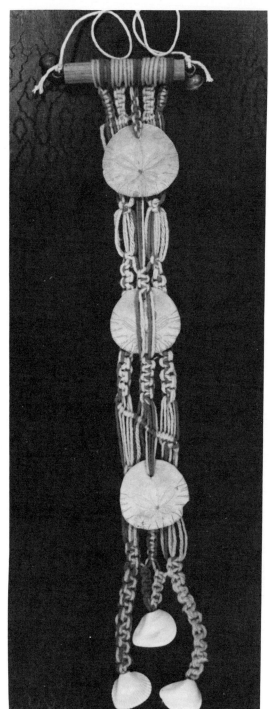

Lesson Objectives

UNDERSTANDING ART (Conceptual)

    a. Learn that macrame is an ancient way of weaving and that sailors used to do it. (C)

    b. Explain the meaning of macrame as a kind of weaving done by knotting string together in special ways. (B)

MAKING ART (Performance)

    a. Practice making simple macrame knots. (E)

    b. Make a simple shape out of macrame using basic macrame knots. (F)

Art Materials
String of different kinds

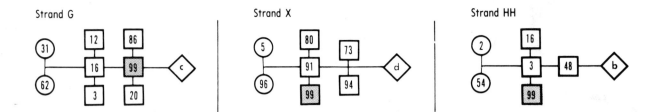

Strand G

Strand X

Strand HH

Lesson 99 — WOMEN ARTISTS

Today women can be seen doing a variety of jobs. In the field of arts, there are women painters, architects, designers, and sculptors. This lesson is to introduce you to some of the women who have become famous artists. You will not do any artwork. Instead you will discuss the artwork of three different women artists.

Instructions

1. Look at the artwork done by women artists in this lesson and in other books. Here is a list of names to look for:

Lee Bontecou
Margaret Bourke-
    White
Mary Cassatt
Lynn Chadwick
Helen Frankenthaler
Grace Hartigan
Barbara Hepworth
Angelica Kauffman

Kathe Kollwitz
Loren MacIvor
Marisol (Escobar)
Berthe Morisot
Louise Nevelson
Georgia O'Keeffe
Bridget Riley
Marie Ann Elisabeth
    Vigee-Lebrun

2. Choose three artworks by different women artists. Choose the ones you can talk about best. Describe each of the artworks. Tell about every detail you can see in them. Explain what you think each is about. If you are not sure, make a guess. You can write your answers or you can talk about the artworks. Your teacher may tell you which he or she prefers for you to do. The color picture by Nancy Singleton (13A) shows work by a woman artist.

Bridget Riley, "Fragments"

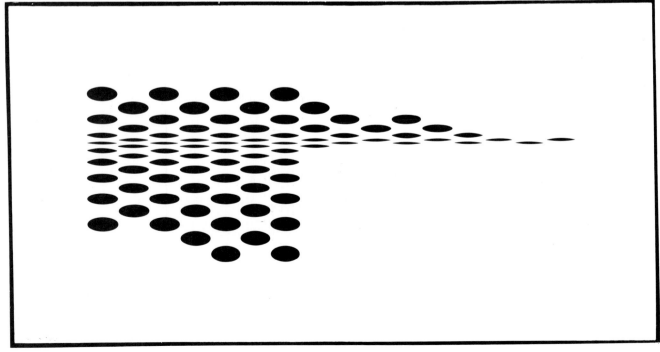

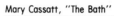
Barbara Hepworth, "Bicentric Form" (2nd view)

Lee Bontecou, "Untitled"

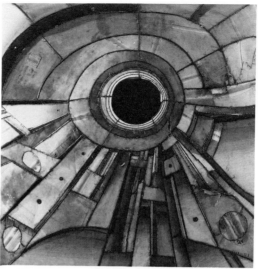

Courtesy of The Art Institute of Chicago

Mary Cassatt, "The Bath"

The Tate Gallery, London

Courtesy of The Art Institute of Chicago

Lesson Objectives

UNDERSTANDING ART (Conceptual)

Learn that art lessons can be done by looking and talking as well as making things. (C)

APPRECIATING ART (Affective)

a. Describe everything you can see in three artworks done by women. (A)

b. Explain what the meaning is of three artworks done by women artists. (D)

Art Materials
Paper and pencil

Strand B

63 — 91 — 100 — ◊ b
6, 47, 60

Strand EE

88 — 37 — ◊ c
52, 33, 100, 50

Lesson 100 — FANCY POTS

Pots are made out of clay. They are baked in a hot oven called a kiln*. When pots come out of the kiln, the clay has been turned into pottery. Some pots are used for cooking food. These shapes are usually simple. Other pots are used for decoration and are made in all kinds of shapes. This lesson is about a piece of pottery that is meant mainly for decoration. You may want it to be useful as well, but the most important thing is to make a pot that shows how good your imagination is.

Instructions

1. There are three main ways of using clay(†) to make pots. The illustrations that go with this lesson show how to do them. Practice doing each of them. This will help you get some ideas.

2. Invent a piece of pottery that shows how creative you are. You can use all of the ways of making pots, or you can use just one or two ways. If there is a kiln in the school, fire* your pot in it when it is perfectly dry.

*The meaning of this word is in the Glossary. (232-236)   † For an explanation turn to the How To Do It section. (237-250)

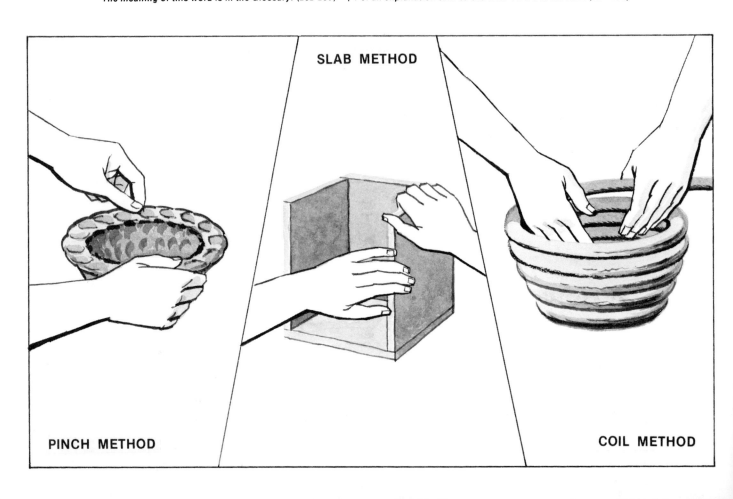

SLAB METHOD

PINCH METHOD

COIL METHOD

Vicki Bodenhamer, "Saddle Bottle"

Aquamanile

Courtesy of the Indiana University Art Museum

Lesson Objectives
UNDERSTANDING ART (Conceptual)
a. Learn that pottery is made by baking clay in a very hot oven called a kiln. (C)
b. Learn that useful shapes are often simpler than ones mainly for decoration. (C)
c. Explain the meaning of fire in art as baking clay to turn it into pottery. (B)

MAKING ART (Performance)
a. Make a decorated pot. (F)
b. Practice the three methods of making pots: by coiling, pinching, and slab. (E)

Art Materials
Clay (water base)
Water, paper towels
Burlap (9" x 12")
Water container
Plastic bag
Modeling stick or nail file
Newspaper
Two pieces of wood
Rolling pin

231

The following guide is used by permission. From Webster's New Collegiate Dictionary, copyright 1973 by G. & C. Merriam Co., Publishers of the Merriam-Webster Dictionaries.

a as in map	i as in tip	s as in less
ā as in day	ī as in side	sh as in shy
ä as in cot	j as in job	t as in tie
à as in father	k as in kin	th as in thin
aů as in out	l as in pool	th as in then
b as in baby	m as in dim	ü as in rule
ch as in chin	n as in no	ů as in pull
d as in did	ŋ as in sing	v as in give
e as in bed	ō as in bone	w as in we
ē as in easy	ò as in saw	y as in yard
f as in cuff	òi as in coin	z as in zone
g as in go	p as in lip	zh as in vision
h as in hat	r as in rarity	ə as in banana, collect

Glossary

abstract /ab-'strakt/ Using only parts of things and changing other parts to make them look unreal. 70, 88

appliqué /ˌap-lə-'kā/ Sewing or gluing cloth pieces or other things to a cloth background to create a design. 114

arch /'ärch/ An opening in a wall to let people or light pass through. 38, 90

architect /'är-kə-ˌtekt/ A person who designs buildings and oversees their construction. 72, 84, 92, 94

architecture /'är-kə-ˌtek-chər/ The art of designing and constructing buildings. 38, 84

armature ('är-mə-chů(ə)r/ A skeleton made of wood, wire, piping, or rolled paper to go inside a sculpture to make it strong. 100

avant-garde /ˌäv-ˌän(t)-'gärd/ People who create new, original ideas. 136

balance /'bal-ən(t)s/ When all the parts of a work of art seem to be equal. 42

bird's-eye view /'bərd-ˌzī-vyü/ Looking down on things the way birds see them. 138

block /'bläk/ Something solid that has a design cut into it. 130

brad /'brad/ A thin nail with a small head. 166

brayer /'brā-ər/ A rubber roller for spreading printing ink evenly. 130

caricature /'kar-i-kə-ˌchů(ə)r/ A picture of someone with some parts exaggerated. 108

carving /'kär-viŋ/ Sculpture made by cutting away unwanted parts. 96, 132

cathedral /kə-'thē-drəl/ A very large and important church. 38, 90

center of interest /'sent-ər əv 'in-trəst/ The most important part of an artwork. 176

clay /'klā/ A powdery kind of earth that can be molded into pottery when wet. 100

collage /kə-'läzh/ An artwork made by gluing different things down on a flat surface. 52

column /'käl-əm/ A round stone post used to support a roof. 38

compass /'kəm-pəs/ A tool with two hinged legs for drawing circles. One leg is pointed; the other holds a pencil. 116

composition /ˌkäm-pə-'zish-ən/ An artwork where all the parts are related. (see unity) 50

contour /'kän-ˌtu̇(ə)r/ The inside and outside edges of any change of shape in an object. 156, 210

create /krē-'āt/ To make something with imagination. 156

creative /krē-'āt-iv/ (see create) 186, 198

creativity /krē-(ˌ)ā-'tiv-ət-ē/ (see create) 132

design /di-'zīn/ A mixture of arranging and inventing in art. 50

distorted /dis-'tȯ(ə)rt-əd/ (see distortion) 158

distortion /dis-'tȯr-shən/ A change in the way something looks to make it more interesting. 98, 171

dome /'dōm/ A curved roof of a building that looks like a ball cut in half horizontally. 38

emboss /im-'bäs/ To decorate with raised designs. 224

embroidery /im-'brȯid-(ə)-rē/ Designs and pictures made by sewing with needle and thread on cloth. Small pictures and clothes are often done in embroidery. 86

fire /'fi(ə)r/ (pottery) The term for baking clay to turn it into pottery. 104, 230

focus /'fō-kəs/ When something is clear and easy to see, it is in focus. When it looks blurred, it is out of focus. 160

freehand /'frē-ˌhand/ Drawing done without any help from tracing paper, rulers, compasses, etc. 98, 202

genius /'jē-nyəs/ Someone who does things much better than anyone else. 154

geodesic dome /ˌjē-ə-'des-ik dōm/ Lightweight dome built of triangular blocks. 72

geometric /ˌjē-ə-'me-trik/ Consisting of straight lines and simple curves, as in geometric shapes or designs. 60, 74, 116

hard-edge /'härd-'ej/ A way of painting with clear, sharp edges. 60

horizon /hə-'rīz-ᵊn/ A level line where water or flat land seems to end and the sky begins. 138

horizontal /ˌhȯr-ə-'zänt-ᵊl/ Flat or level. 204

illustration /ˌil-əs-'trā-shən/ Designs and pictures that explain things or show what happened in a story. 198

invent /in-'vent/ To do something for the first time. 198

kiln /'kiln/ A special oven used for making pottery. 230

lacquer /'lak-ər/ A very hard, shiny paint. 224

landscape /'lan(d)-ˌskāp/ A picture made of an outdoor scene. 54, 62, 66

loom /'lüm/ Any type of framework used for weaving. 68

macrame /ˌmak-rə-'mā/ A kind of weaving done by tying knots in string. 226

magnify /'mag-nə-ˌfī/ To make something look bigger. 82

magnifying glass /'mag-nə-ˌfī-iŋ glas/ A lens that makes things look larger. 78

microscope /'mī-krə-ˌskōp/ An instrument that magnifies things too small to be seen clearly with the human eye. 78, 82

mobile /'mō-ˌbēl/ A kind of hanging sculpture that has many balanced parts. 76

module /'mäj-(ˌ)ü(ə)l/ A simple solid object used over and over again to make an artwork. 168

monochrome /'män-ə-krōm/ A painting with only one hue (color). Changes are possible only with the addition of black and/or white. 34

negative /'neg-ət-iv/ (photography) A picture that shows colors and shades that are opposite of what is normal. 182

original /ə-'rig-ən-əl/ Ideas in art that are very unusual or different. Original can also mean a real work of art and not a copy. 48, 104

outline /'aut-ˌlīn/ The line drawn around the outside edge of a shape. 162

pillar /'pil-ər/ A post made of stone that holds up the roof of a building. 102

plaster /'plas-tər/ A white powder mixed with water that hardens when dry. 100

portrait /'pōr-trət/ A work of art that shows the face of a person. 188

positive /'päz-ət-iv/ (photography) A picture that shows colors and shades as we see them. 182

proportion /p(r)ə-'pōr-shən/ The size measurement of one thing compared with the size measurement of another thing. 128

protractor /prō-'trak-tər/ A piece of wood or plastic shaped in a half or full circle used for measuring angles. 116

rasp /'rasp/ A file with rough teeth used for wood or plaster. 97

ratio /'rā-shō/ The measurement of one thing compared with another. 128

reflection /ri-'flek-shən/ An image thrown back, as from still water or a mirror. 204

relief /ri-'lēf/ A kind of art that sticks out from a flat background. It is halfway between a flat picture and a solid sculpture. 42, 48, 156, 224

sculpture /'skəlp-chər/ Art that is solid. 96, 106

sequin /'sē-kwən/ A small, shiny metal circle that can be stitched to cloth. 86

set square /'set 'skwa(ə)r/ A wood or plastic triangle used in technical drawing. 116

silhouette /ˌsil-ə-'wet/ The solid shape of something that looks like a shadow with no details inside. It is usually all black or white. 140

skyscraper /'skī-ˌskrā-pər/ A very tall building. 72, 84

space /'spās/ All the open parts in or between shapes. 40

steeple /'stē-pəl/ A pointed tower on top of a church. 90

stitchery /stitch-ə-rē/ A way of making art using wool, thread, etc. on a cloth background. 74, 86

style /'stī(ə)l/ The special way each artist does his or her work. 192, 194

symmetrical /sə-'me-tri-kəl/ (see symmetry) 42

symmetry /'sim-ə-trē/ A kind of balance where the things on each side of a center line are the same. 42

tapestry /'tap-ə-strē/ A picture that is woven in cloth and hung on a wall. 86

template /'tem-plət/ A shape used as a guide to draw shapes neatly and exactly alike. 116

textile /'tek-ˌstīl/ A woven fabric. 226

texture /'teks-chər/ The way a surface looks or feels - rough, smooth, silky, etc. 56

title /'tīt-əl/ The name given to a picture or piece of artwork. 46, 58, 208

transfer /tran(t)s-'fər/ To move a drawing or design from one surface to another. 130

transparent /tran(t)s-'par-ənt/ Being able to see through something clearly, like looking through glass. 66

T square /tē skwa(ə)r/ A long straight edge attached to a short cross piece which slides along the edge of a drawing board. 116

unity /'yü-nət-ē/ When all the parts of a work of art look as though they belong together. 42

vertical /'vərt-i-kəl/ Straight up and down. 204

wall hanging /'wȯl 'haŋ-iŋ/ An artwork hung from a wall for decoration. 114

warp /'wȯ(ə)rp/ Vertical threading of a loom. These are the threads through which the weft is woven. 68

watercolor /'wȯt-ər-ˌkəl-ər/ A kind of paint made with powder mixed with glue and water. It is best used thinly (see transparent). It usually comes in solid blocks in paint boxes. 50

weaving /'wēv-iŋ/ The interlacing of yarn to make cloth. 68

weft /'weft/ The thread, yarn, etc. that is woven back and forth across the warp thread to make the visible design of a textile. 68

yarn /'yärn/ A strand-like material made of cotton, wool, or synthetic material. It is used mainly for stitchery, weaving, and appliqué. 74

HOW TO DO IT

DRAWING. In most schools there are pencils to draw with. You can also draw with crayons and oil pastels. Some schools will have pens and ink for drawing. Rulers are also useful in art and so are pencil compasses. And everyone should know how to make a tracing.

Pencils. The best pencils for art have fairly soft leads. Soft pencils have thick leads. If you press hard with a soft pencil, it will make black lines and shading. If you lift up a little it will make gray lines and shadings.

You can fill in a shape solidly to shade it. You can also shade in with lines.

Crayons and Oil Pastels. Crayons are hard and waxy. Oil pastels are softer and make brighter colors. They smudge more easily than crayons. You can draw with the points or unwrap them and use the sides. If you press hard, the colors will be bright. If you don't press hard, the colors will be lighter. Rough paper makes the colors lighter. Smoother paper makes them brighter. You can mix colors together by adding one color over another. Another way is to put dots of different colors side by side.

Pen and Ink. Pen points [or pen nibs] come in different shapes and sizes and make different kinds of lines. But with all of them remember never to push the point away from you. It will dig into the paper and splatter ink. The best way to use a pen is to draw on a sloping surface; be sure there is not too much ink in the pen.

Drawing ink comes in two varieties — waterproof and non-waterproof. Waterproof inks look best but are difficult to remove if accidentally spilled.

Using a Ruler. A ruler has a straight edge and is marked out for measuring. To draw a straight line, hold the ruler firmly on a piece of paper and press the side of the pencil against the ruler as you slide the pencil point over the paper.

If you need to draw lines of an exact length, hold the ruler in place and make pencil dots to show the beginning and end of the line. Then draw the line from the first dot to the second one in the same way as you did before.

If you are not used to doing this, practice drawing lines of these exact lengths: 2″, 5″, 9″, 11″, 7½″, 3½″, 10¾″, and 5¾″.

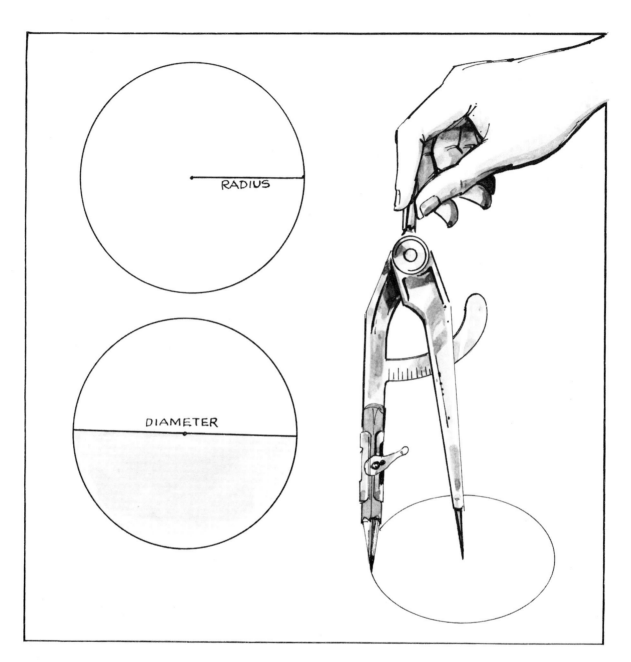

Using a Pencil Compass. A pencil compass has two legs. One leg has a point at the end. The other leg is made so it will hold a pencil. Before you begin, be sure the legs are fairly tight and will not move easily. Also be sure the pencil will stay in the holder without slipping. The pencil should stick out to make both legs about equal in length.

To draw a circle or part of a circle, spread the two legs apart. Press the metal point into the paper. Keep the hole as small as possible.

* The meaning of this word is in the Glossary. (232-236)

Now hold the pencil around the top and turn the leg holding the pencil around the pointed leg. You will draw a perfect circle.

Practice drawing circles and parts of circles. The measurement from the center of a circle to the outside edge is called the radius*. What is the radius of the biggest circle you can draw with your compass? What is the smallest radius? The distance all the way across a circle is the diameter*. Can you draw a circle with a diameter of 10 centimeters?

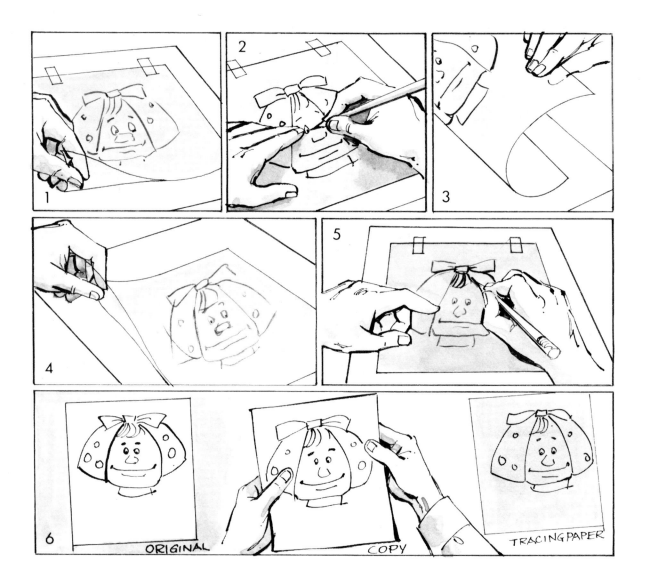

Tracing. Tracing is a quick way to draw something exactly. It is useful when you want to repeat something you have already done. You can also learn about how things look by tracing them. Follow these instructions.

1. Place a piece of tracing paper on top of the thing you want to trace. Hold the two pieces of paper together with paper clips or tape.

2. Draw on the tracing paper to show all the lines you want in the drawing underneath.

3. Remove the tracing paper. Turn it over. Put it on a pad of newspaper. Use a blunt pencil point or scribble with the side of the lead. Cover the lines thickly.

4. Turn the tracing paper the right way over again. Put it on top of a clean piece of drawing paper.

5. Keep the drawing paper and the tracing paper together with paper clips, pins, or tape. Draw over the lines on the tracing paper again.

6. Remove the tracing paper. The lines should now show on the drawing paper. You may need to draw over some of them again to make them really clear.

240

PAINTING. School paints are usually the kind that mix with water. There are two main kinds of school paints. One works best when it is like thick cream. It is called tempera*. The other is best used thinly and is called watercolor*.

Tempera Paint. Tempera colors come as powder, liquid, and solid blocks of color.

Powder paint comes in cans or boxes. It has to be mixed carefully a little at a time. Keep adding water and powder until you have enough paint. Only mix as much powder color as you need. If it dries in the paint tray, it usually cannot be used again.

Liquid tempera comes in a jar, tubes, and plastic containers. It is usually ready to be

The meaning of this word is in the Glossary. (232-236)

spooned out into paint trays. If it has been stored for a long time, it may have to be stirred first. Be sure that any sticks, brushes, or spoons you use are always clean. Then you will not dirty the paint and spoil it. Keep the lids on when the paint is not being used. And keep paint cleaned out of the cap so it will not dry out and stick. If a bottle cap does stick, it will usually loosen in warm water.

Tempera blocks or cakes are made to dissolve easily when rubbed gently with a wet brush. Large blocks come separately. Small blocks of different colors come together in paint boxes.

Be sure to remember that tempera paint looks best when it is thick and creamy. You should not be able to see through to the paper underneath. It is opaque* paint.

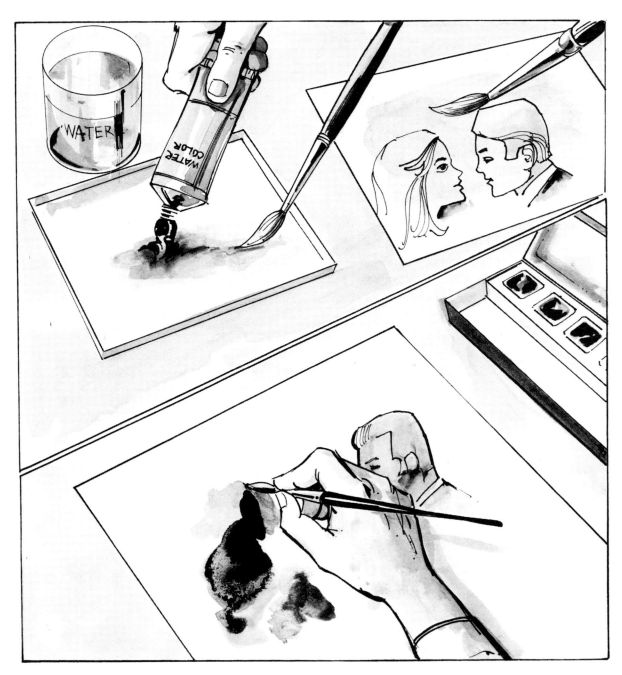

Watercolor Paint. These paints come either in tubes or in small solid pans or cakes. The solid paint dissolves very easily when it is rubbed with a wet brush. This kind of paint is meant to be used thinly and with plenty of water. You should also be able to see through it to the paper underneath. It is transparent* paint.

Color Mixing. Most art looks better if you mix colors together. Here are some ways to mix the colors you want. You will need some paints, brushes, a mixing tray, a water can or jar, a cloth or some paper towels, and paper to paint on.

Important: Keep the water in your water can clean. Wash your brush before dipping into a new color.

The meaning of this word is in the Glossary. (232-236)

242

How to Mix a Color: Follow these instructions whenever you mix colors together.

Useful Hints

1. With tempera paint, always start your mixing with light colors and add darker colors to them — a little at a time. Be very careful not to use a lot of black.

2. Never try to lighten tempera paint that has become too dark. You will have to use the color as it is or throw it away.

3. To mix green add blue to yellow.

4. To mix orange add red to yellow.

5. To mix violet add blue to red.

6. To mix brown try putting these colors together: a) red and green
    b) red, yellow, and black
    c) red and black

7. To mix gray add black tempera to white. With watercolors just thin down some black paint with water. All grays look better with a dab of another color added.

8. To make watercolors lighter, add water.

9. To make watercolors darker, use less water.

PAPER. Hundreds of different kinds of paper are made, but five kinds are used most often for school art. Drawings look best on fairly thick, white paper that is not too smooth. One kind of drawing paper is called manila. Quality paper is often called drawing paper. You can paint on drawing paper. It can also be used for paper sculpture if it is thick enough. Construction paper is another kind of school paper. It usually comes in different colors and is used for tempera painting, collage, and paper sculpture. Newsprint paper is like a newspaper without the printing on it. It is inexpensive and it tears easily, but it is very good for doing sketch ideas in art, printing, and making papier-mâché.

Tissue paper is very thin and strong. Colored tissue paper is good for making collages. Tracing paper is just used to make tracings. You can see through it. It tears easily.

Here are the names of other kinds of paper you can use in school artwork: bogus, butcher, corrugated, crepe, graph, kraft, tagboard, charcoal, and watercolor.

Folding. Bend the paper so that one edge is exactly on top of the other. Hold the two edges together. Smooth the paper until it creases at the center. Then crease the fold between your finger and thumb.

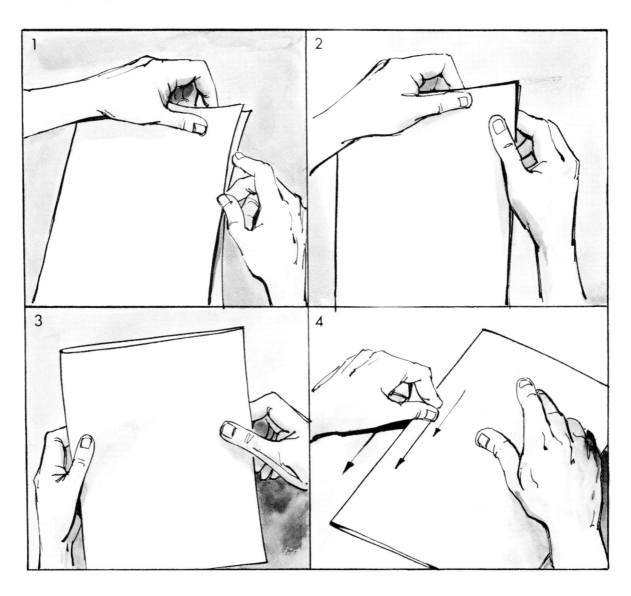

Tearing. One kind of tearing is done just by tearing paper apart with your hands. Paper will usually tear more easily in one direction than another. The edges will look ragged and fuzzy.

Another kind of tearing is in straight lines. First you fold and crease a sheet of paper. Open it flat again. Place one hand flat near the top of the crease. Take hold of the top corner with the other hand. Pull outwards and downwards and the paper will tear along the creased fold. As you tear, keep both hands about opposite each other. If you do not, the paper will not tear along the crease.

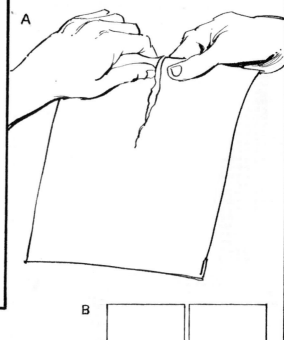

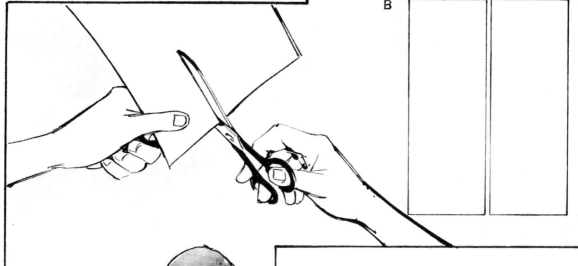

Cutting. The easiest way to cut paper is to use scissors. If you have not used scissors for a long time, look at these pictures.

Important: Remember not to waste paper. Always cut what you need from the edge of a sheet of paper and not from the center.

You can also cut with a paper cutter. It makes straight cuts only. It can cut several sheets at once depending on how thick the paper is. Hold the paper down firmly when you cut. Be sure your fingers are out of the way when you bring the blade down.

GLUE, PASTE, AND CEMENT. School paste is thick, soft, and white and usually comes in jars. It is sometimes called library paste. It is good for sticking paper and cardboard. Wheat paste is a powder. It comes in packages and must be mixed with water. Follow the instructions carefully and do not mix more paste than you need. Some powdered pastes mix into very large quantities. It is good for sticking paper and cardboard. White glue is a white, creamy liquid. It comes in plastic squeeze bottles and in large containers. It is best used to stick cardboard, wood, cloth, styrofoam, and pottery. Rubber cement comes in tubes, bottles, and cans. It dries very quickly so always keep the cap on tightly. Paper does not wrinkle when it is stuck with rubber cement.

How to Stick Things Together: Spread out some newspaper. Place the artwork you want to stick face downwards. Spread the glue, paste, or cement outwards from the center. Use a spreader, brush, or your finger. Be sure the edges and corners are all covered. Lift the paper up and place it where it is supposed to go. Smooth the paper flat with clean hands. You can place a sheet of paper over the top and smooth down on top of that.

Important: Always use the least amount of glue. Too much will spoil your work. If you use a brush, be sure to wash white glue out of it with water before it dries. Rubber cement brushes must go back into the cement bottle to keep soft or be washed in special thinners. Remember that both dry very quickly. Always clean up thoroughly after using paste, glue, or cement.

PAPIER-MÂCHÉ. This is a kind of modeling clay made out of paper and glue. It is made in two ways. One is called pulp. The other is called strip.

Preparing Pulp. Soak small pieces of soft paper, like newsprint, newspaper, facial tissue, etc., in water. Squeeze out the extra water. Thoroughly mix in some school paste or mixed-up wheat paste. Let the pulp stand for an hour or two before working on it.

Preparing Strip. Soak torn or cut strips of newsprint or newspaper in water. Squeeze out the extra water. Put down a layer of wet strips over the shape you want to cover. Then paste down a second layer of strips to cover the first layer. If you began with white, the second layer should be colored. Next you paste down another layer of the opposite color. You will normally need to make the papier-mâché five or six layers thick.

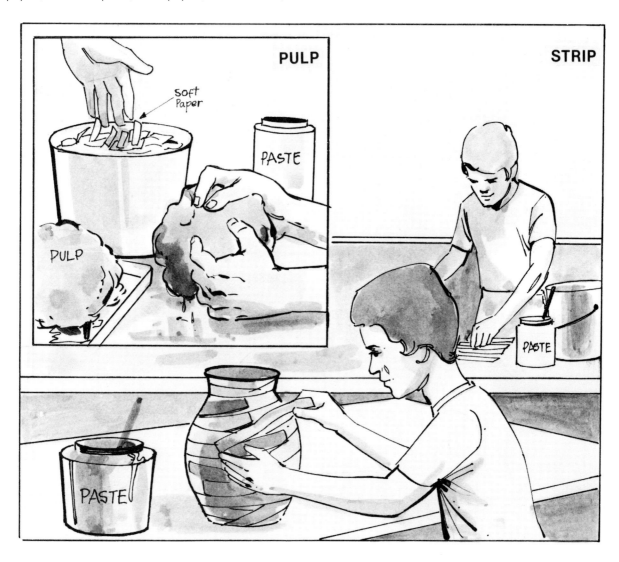

MOUNTING ARTWORK. Your work will look better if it has a frame around it. The simplest kind of frame is called a mount*. Put a small dab of paste at each corner of your work. Then place it on a sheet of construction paper or cardboard that is bigger on all sides than your work. The construction paper should be a color that makes your work look good. A border of 2″ to 3″ is good. The border can be slightly narrower at the top and slightly wider at the bottom.

The meaning of this word is in the Glossary. (232-236)

CLAY. There are two kinds of commonly used clay. One is mixed with water and is called **water-based clay***. It is usually a gray or a reddish-brown color and it comes as a powder or ready-mixed. The other is mixed with linseed oil and is called oil-based clay*.

Preparing Water-Based Clay. If clay comes as a powder, your teacher must supervise the mixing. If the clay is already mixed, it will be in a plastic sack and will be ready to use. To keep water-based clay in good condition, keep your hands wet with water as you work.

If the clay is to be used for pottery, any air bubbles in it must be removed. This is **called wedging***. The easiest way to wedge is to throw some clay onto a desk top covered with newspaper. Tear it in two and pound the pieces together. Then throw it down again. This knocks the air bubbles out.

To keep water-based clay from one class period to the next, put it into a plastic sack and tie the end tight. If you do not have plastic sacks, wrap the clay in old cloths that are soaking wet, and keep them wet.

Joining Clay Together. When you join two pieces of water-based clay together, each piece should be about as wet as the other. Scratch the edges to be joined. Paint these pieces with a creamy mixture of clay and water, called slip*, and press them together. If the clay has dried out a little, then make the slip with vinegar instead of water.

Important: Always check with your teacher before letting any slip run down the drain. It can block the piping.

* The meaning of this word is in the Glossary. (232-236)

Preparing Oil-Based Clay. Oil-based clay comes in all kinds of colors and is always ready-mixed. All you have to do is squeeze it and twist it. The warmth of your hands makes it soft. It is easy to use and it sticks together. It does not dry out hard like water-based clay. It can be used over and over again. But it cannot be made into pottery. After a long time the clay loses most of the oil and is difficult to make soft. It either sets very hard or crumbles to pieces.

PLASTER OF PARIS. Plaster is a very white powder and comes in large paper sacks. After being mixed with water it quickly turns solid. It must be kept dry before use; otherwise it will not turn solid when you want it to.

How to Mix Plaster: Put some water in a bowl or bucket. Your teacher will tell you how much you need. Sprinkle plaster quickly into the water until it begins to show through the surface of the water. Then mix the plaster and water together thoroughly with your hands.

When the plaster begins to thicken, it is ready to pour. Plaster thickens quite quickly. It becomes nice and warm as it sets hard. Always be sure to leave plaster alone until it is perfectly dry.

Important: Always put plaster that is to be thrown away in a special garbage can. It must never be put down the drain. Plaster can be messy, so keep your space clean when using it.

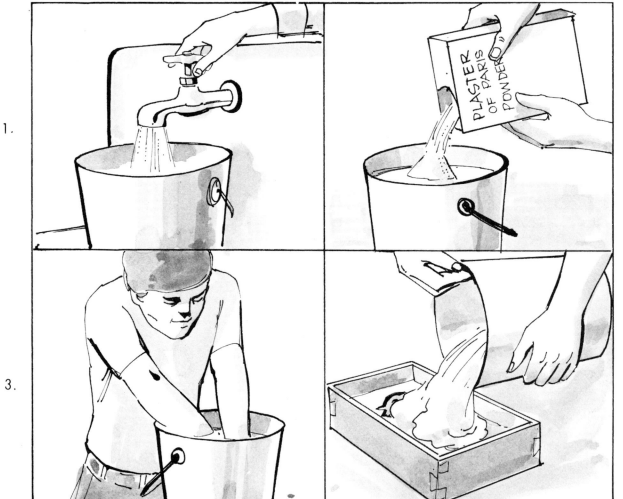

1.

2.

3.

4.

INDEX OF ART YOU WANT TO DO

Acknowledgments

Our thanks to the following for permission to reproduce the art and photographs that appear on the pages indicated:

Illustrators, Luis Machare, 12, 86, 120, 128, 230, 237-250

Richard Wahl, 52, 59, 60 (left), 77, 100, 126, 127, 131, 162, 163, 177, 185, 199, 226

Alvarado, Omar, 178 (right), Andersen, Hans, 120, Anderson, Warren, 179 (top), Artemisia Gallery, Chicago, 125

Ball State University Photo Service, 187 (right)

The Bead Box, Bloomington, IN, 104, 105, 227 (left)

The British Tourist Authority, 90, 121 (bottom)

Cabanban, Orlando R., 85 (top right)

City of Chicago, Department of Streets and Sanitation, 194 (right)

Consulate General of Japan, 95 (bottom left)

Crewell, Larry, 175

Department of Public Relations, City of Montreal, Canada, 73 (top right), 148

Eboigbe, Felix, 133 (bottom and left)

The Field Museum of Natural History, 119 (top right)

First Federal Savings and Loan Association of Chicago, 122

Fox, Amy, Oak Hill Jr. High School, Converse, IN, 116

French Government Tourist Office, 149 (bottom right)

Greek National Tourist Office, 39 (top)

Heeg, John, St. Anne's School, Archdiocese of Cincinnati, OH, 137 (bottom left)

Hickey, Denise, 94, Hoffman, Judy, 180, Hradecky, Penny, 118, Hyatt Regency Hotel, San Francisco, 41

Indiana University, 236 (top right, center right), Audio Visual Photo Lab, 40, Department of Zoology, Dr. F. R. Turner, 82, 83

International Collection of Child Art, 51 (bottom right), 113, 130, 138, 147 (bottom), 170, 174 (top), 175 (bottom)

Italian Government Travel Office, 38

Jenkins, Crystal, Columbus East High School, Columbus, IN, 224

John G. Shedd Aquarium, Chicago, 119 (bottom left, bottom right)

John Hancock Mutual Life Insurance Company, owner/developer of John Hancock Center, 85 (bottom)

Jordan, Jack, 212, Kaminsky, David, 157

Louisiana Tourist Development Commission, 110, 111, 123

Magic Brandt, 80, 112, 113, 116, 182, 183, 187 (bottom), 198 (left), 200 (left), 204, 227 (top left)

   Eastwood Jr. High School, Indianapolis, IN, Eric Brass, 153 (top left), Stephanie Kennedy, 157, Carolyn Kohlbecker, 153 (top right)

   Thomas Jefferson Jr. High School, Cleveland, OH, Sharon Carey, 188, Tami Pusil, 189 (right)

   Oak Hill Jr. High School, Converse, IN, Roger Vogel, 99 (right)

Marvel Comics, 146, 218 (left)

Moore, Michael Fred, 42, 56 (right), 69, 125, 159, 165, 168, 173, 198 (right), 210, 211

National Aeronautics and Space Administration, 140, 201

The National Trust, 91 (right)

Nickel, Richard, for the Commission on Chicago Landmarks, 73 (bottom), 84

Osterhoudt, Harvey, 56 (left), 75 (bottom), 96, 97, 104, 105, 106, 156, 186, 200 (right), 227 (bottom and right)

   Bedford Jr. High School, IN, Jeremy Wilbur, 133 (top)

   Eastwood Jr. High School, Indianapolis, IN, Donnie Arbogast, 49, Belinda Haney, 167 (right), Angela Longerbone, 115, Ruth Masley, 98, 99 (top left), Miki Mottler, 60 (right), Marie Shaver, 124, John Lanier, 153 (bottom left)

   Glenwood Jr. High School, Findley, OH, Greg Coles, 172

   R. H. Jamison Jr. High School, Cleveland, OH, Dovie Jones, 53 (top), Opendella Williams, 53 (bottom)

   Northside Jr. High School, Columbus, IN, Eric Clark, 225 (right)

   Westlane Jr. High School, Indianapolis, IN, Michael Hinkle, 108 (left)

   Tya Hanna, 97 (top left), Mike Masar, 96, Lynn Steinkamp, 97 (bottom)

Peak, Len, 78, 79, 145, 160, 161

Remular, Marino, Waipahu Intermediate School, Waipahu, HA, 197 (bottom right)

Rito, Georgiana, 119 (top left)

School Arts, 97

   Maple Dale School, Fox Point, WI, Brian Baumann, 166

   Clinton Place Jr. High School, Newark, NJ, Eason Evans, 46

   Bay Middle School, Bay Village, OH, Susan Shriver, 68

   John Kohler, 97 (top right), John Kroth, 149 (top right)

Sears, Roebuck and Company, 85 (top Left), Shalliol, David, 132, Shulman, Julius, 149 (left)

Talbot Studios, Bloomington, IN, 43, 51 (top right)

Trans World Airlines, 91 (left), United Air Lines, 121 (top)

United States Department of the Interior, 36 (upper right), 36 (left)

University of Virginia, Monticello, VI, 72

Wallace, Bob, 87

Yale University Department of Public Information, 95 (bottom right)

Yates, Glenda, L. V. Rogers High School, Nelson, B.C., Canada, 129 (left)